AF395157

Praise for The Brand Building Playbook

Venture building starts with brand building. If that's not your expertise, this terrific entrepreneur will hold your hand every step of the way. He shows you - in simple, friendly language – the logic and importance of every single step.

Bob Dorf, Author of The Startup Owner's Manual

Buy this book. It teaches you how to build an effective message in a world that has a hard time listening.

Joachim Blazer, Author of The #1 Guide to Startup Valuation

I strongly advise anyone who is launching a new venture to buy this book and build a brand that works.

Vincent Karremans, Founder & CEO Magnet.me

If you want to play the game, you've got to know the rules. Wouter's guide is clear and cutthroat at times; a guide on how to achieve your own personal success in a particular arena. There's a wealth of information, so choose the ones you feel are true to your heart, and make the brand an expression of you. Trust the process. Be true to your brand, and the right audience will follow!

Georgios-Ioannis Tsianos, Super athlete & speaker

Building powerful brands used to be the domain of a select few. This book makes it possible for everyone. It helps you win - no matter the project, no matter the market.

Wilbert Kannekens, Founder & CEO Toby

The Brand Building Playbook

A Guide With Easy Steps for Every Budget

Wouter Frederik Chömpff

BRANDBUILDING.COM

BrandBuilding.com
Hovenierskade 16
2805 PK, Gouda, The Netherlands
hello@brandbuilding.com
www.brandbuilding.com

Published by BrandBuilding.com 2019

Special discounts are available on quantity purchases by corporations,
associations, and others. The author is available as a speaker, consultant
and trainer. For details, contact the publisher at the address above.

This hardcover edition is printed on demand.

ISBN 9 789 083 024 929

To family.

Contents

Preface – A multimillion-dollar education

So, you've built something special?

And you're ready to destroy the competition?

You and your project.　　　　Your competition (a.k.a. yesterday's fools).

Think again.

The odds are stacked against you. Every single day, the world greets 250,000 new businesses, 5,000 new books, and 6,000 new mobile apps[1]. And everyone hopes their project will be a smashing success. Of course not.

Almost every project fails.

No.　　　　Nope.　　　　No way.　　　　Never mind.

The reason for failure is always the same:

People don't buy, use, donate to, invest in or vote for the project.

In short: not enough people commit. The project simply isn't valuable enough to spend their time, money or attention.

This is very common. The market is saturated with starry-eyed entrepreneurs, writers, and app developers hoping to make it big.

Yet they all have the same challenge:

Every project has to communicate its value. And that's very hard.

That's why I wrote this book. You've put a lot of effort into building something special. You believe in your project, all the way. But you must learn to communicate its value if you want others to commit.

And communicating value is what brand building is all about.

How do you present your project to a skeptical audience? How do you convince others of its usefulness? How do you get it ready for a brutally competitive market? Tough questions.

I feel you, for I've walked that very same road — many times.

And I could've used a guide. For over a decade, I've been building brands for myself and others, making all the mistakes one can make. But even though building brands is hard, I figured it out eventually.

So, here's the book I needed 15 years ago. I burned through millions of (mostly other people's) dollars discovering its lessons.

Let's write a book about this stuff!

It was an extravagant education, but worth sharing in this book.

I hope it arrived in time for you.

Acknowledgements

I grossly underestimated the difficulty of writing a book worth reading.

Luckily, the people around me helped me make it happen.
You have my deepest, heartfelt gratitude.

To my wife Sharon, who believed in me even before I had pennies to rub together. Thank you for your love and support.

To my daughters, who saw their father leave for the library many evenings and weekends. Thank you for the joyful reception upon each return.

To my savage brothers, who absolutely crucified the drafts of this book. Thank you for your faith and friendship.

To my parents, who brewed up a perfect youth. Thank you for your enduring love and generosity.

To my grandmother, who taught me many things, including French and French living. Thank you for a joyous example of immortality.

To Hans Westerhof, who supported my entrepreneurial efforts since 2014. Thank you for your help at each critical juncture.

To Rogier van Mazijk en Jan-Matthijs de Berg, who took me on some strange journeys. Thanks for providing unlimited food for thought.

To Bob Dorf, who was willing to befriend two outsiders whilst adventuring in Greece. Thank you for sending the elevator down.

To Joachim Blazer, who showed me the possibility of writing and publishing a succesful book. Thank you for this ambitious beacon.

And to you, the buyer of this book. Thank you for your patronage and goodwill. I hope this guide helps make your dreams come true.

1. Introduction

1.1. Sh*tstained cows don't sell

Why did a hick from the heartland write a book on branding?

That's an easy question. I love branding. I love it more than my hometown.

Besides, my time between the cows taught me the essence of branding:

Sh*tstained cows don't sell.

Wanna try?

Granted. This sounds less profound than your average Steve Jobs quote.

But it's true. Why? Because building a brand is about convincing folks.

And sh*tstains don't help.

You must polish your cow if you want to convince people.

That's the spirit!

That's all there is to it.

Yes, I know that you're not selling cows. (Ranchers don't read.)

The cow polishing is an analogy.

Wax on. Wax off.

Let me clarify.

Cow means your project.

This can be your product, business, charity, person or party. But the word project simplifies things.

Polish means building a brand.

And building a brand is making sure your stuff says the right things.

What is this *stuff*? Good question.

Everything representing your project, from your name and logo to your packaging and personnel.

What are these *right things*? Simple.

That which makes people think your cow – I mean project - is valuable.

1.2. How your brand creates value

There once was a Roman who said that "everything is worth what its purchaser will pay for it". He meant that value is subjective, dependent on the thinking of the buyer.

If someone has a problem, and they think you can fix it - your project is valuable to them. The more useful they think you are, the more valuable you are.

In other words, people think your project is useful when they think your project can help them.

Value = people thinking you are useful.

Cow buyers need quality meat. Donors need happy feelings. Voters need representation. These needs can make your project useful to them. If they don't feel your project will meet their needs, they will not buy, donate to, or vote for it.

Now that's where your brand comes in. By making it say the right things:

Your brand makes people perceive your project as useful.

Now *that* looks yummy!

Cows should be perceived as tasty. Charities should be perceived as effective. Politicians should be perceived as having a voter's interest at heart.

As our Roman implied, this perception is subjective. But subjectivity is what makes branding fun.

And being able to influence perception makes brand builders powerful people. So if you do it right:

Your brand increases the value (perceived usefulness) of your project.

Let me put that in an algebraic function for you:

Project	Brand builder (you)	Valuable project

Same cow, better value. And valuable projects succeed better.

- ✓ Valuable products sell more.
- ✓ Valuable charities receive more donations.
- ✓ Valuable politicians get more votes.

You get the point. Brands are built to promote everything, from cars and candidates to careers. That's why you can use this book for everything you want to be perceived as valuable.

1.3. Why brands are so powerful

By now, you might think a great brand is everything. With the right brand:

- ✓ A sugary soda - best used to declog the sink -
  promises an adventurous life full of sensual surprises.
- ✓ A chemical lipstick – advertised by a bone-thin teenage model –
  promises to keep your date interested beyond the first night.
- ✓ A 4x4 - with the fuel economy of a perforated battle tank –
  promises a major upgrade in masculinity.

As you know, these brand promises are not always fulfilled.

"Still don't feel like the most interesting man in the world…"

Strong brands make everything seem valuable.

This means you can make good money, even if your project is useless. (Think AAA-rated sub-prime mortgages from big-name banks.)

Yet others, by being actually useful, succeed with a weak brand or without a brand. (Think most forms of craftsmanship.)

Let's summarize this in a fancy quadrant and classify projects based on actual and perceived usefulness.

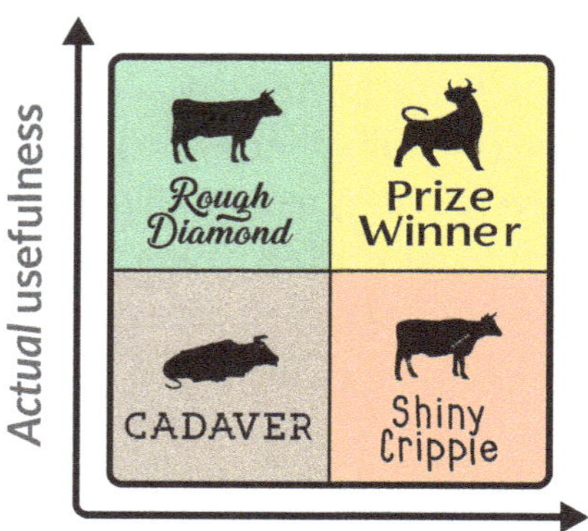

 **Cadavers** languish in anonymity, and for good reason. They aren't useful, nor perceived as such. You won't survive long selling them, so examples are limited to failed start-ups and temporary sweatshops.

 **Shiny cripples** offer little, yet seem valuable somehow. Like that blood test that only required a drop to decide if you needed a doctor but didn't. (Beware: selling shiny cripples can land you in jail and/or hell.)

 **Rough diamonds** are rare, like custom furniture. There's no logo, brochure or website of the master carpenter. Yet that robust chair will be handed down for generations.

 **Prize-winners** are destined for greatness. Both this book and the device on which you are reading it might be examples. It fulfills your needs and looks very shiny.

The lesson of this quadrant is as simple as my inbred cousin:

Every project benefits from a strong brand.

But know this: if your project only pretends to solve a need when it doesn't, you're in trouble. Your support team is flooded with complaints. Angry reviews accumulate online. And the word spreads faster than a fat kid chasing the ice-cream truck.

This negativity affects the strength of your brand. And in my town, folks will tan your hide if you sell a shiny cripple. Remember what happened to the bankers after the financial crisis?

Forget it, bad example.

Let's hope karma comes with interest.

Remember what happened to Theranos after shamming the sick? Exactly.

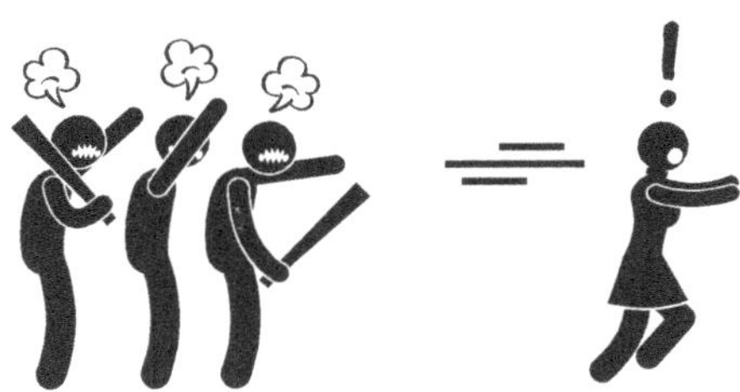

Unfulfilled promises make angry people.

Make sure your project fulfills the promise made by your brand.

Now this book helps you build a strong brand. But like kitchen knives employed for murder, the same tools can be used for evil. You can inflate your project and lure people with useless stuff. This is always unethical and often unlawful.

Don't do it. Things will get really nasty, real fast.

1.4. Why another book on branding?

Why use this book and not so-and-so's? Because:

Classic branding books cater to brand managers, not to brand builders.

I know. I (was forced to) read all of them.

Me reading books so you don't have to.

Reading these books acquaint you with some pieces of the branding puzzle.

Writing them will get you speaking gigs at respectable companies.

Yet they're useless if you need to build a brand. For where do you begin if you're starting from scratch? Or if you lack time, money and experience?

To paraphrase Nassim Taleb:

"The only thing a brand building professor can teach you is how to become a brand building professor."

Also: Classic branding books are impractical or boring.

Some authors highlight only one piece of the puzzle. They focus on their hobbyhorse, leaving you with some crumbs but nothing to sustain a full branding journey.

Others aim to build academic credentials. They recycle platitudes and stuff them with jargon, citations, and pomp. These attempts to bore you to death are borderline criminal.

Go ahead, try one.

As I already made my money and care little for my academic reputation, I tried to avoid the sins of my predecessors. Therefore:

I made this book as practical and entertaining as possible.

It gives you insights into the nature and psychology of branding, as well as a roadmap on creating a strong brand, regardless of your (paltry) experience and (pitiful) budget.

I also included some stick figures. You're welcome.

1.5. Why build your own brand?

A fat wallet might tempt you to trash this book and dump the entire circus with a branding agency. After all, they promise the same as me: help communicate the value of your project. Yet:

Delegating your branding to an agency costs (heaps of) money.

However – despite what their fee suggests – agency folk don't have any magical abilities.

Don't be fooled by turtlenecks, man buns and MacBook's. As in any job, these are merely parts of the uniform your expert uses to signal her supposed competence.

Would you trust:

A lawyer in shorts?	A doctor in a hawaii shirt?	A car salesman with a Christmas tie?

But even if they are competent and affordable, there are more insidious consequences of not building your own brand:

Delegating brand building to an agency means losing stewardship.

When an agency handles research, strategy, design, and advertising, they build up the knowledge and feeling with your brand, removing it from your company. If you pay others to build a brand, you'll never learn to do it yourself.

Delegating brand building to an agency is cumbersome.

For every tiny change, you'll need to call the account manager, who then informs you that the relevant designer is hiking the Appalachian Trail for the coming weeks. Bah. You'll have enough delays within your own team.

So, why go through the effort of reading this book and learning its techniques yourself? Simple:

Hiring agencies means losing (1) money (2) stewardship and (3) time.

Do *not* use

Always build your own brand. Then even if you delegate tasks to outside experts, you've got a firm grip on them and no-one can sell you any bullsh*t.

Finally, there is a rule born from ancient warfare:

Never trust mercenaries to hold your strategic positions.

The same goes for your most crucial asset: your brand. And who cares more about it than you? Here's a hint. NOT the guy charging by the hour.

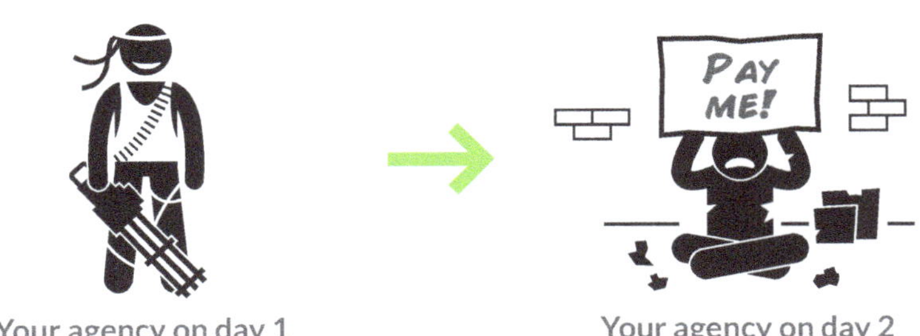

Your agency on day 1   Your agency on day 2

So be brave and do it yourself.

I promise:

You don't need a master's degree in marketing to be good at it. I know, for I've got one. And it's as useless as tits on a bull. (I only advertise my degrees for branding purposes.)

You with
this book.

You with
a degree in whatever.

All you need is an understanding of the principles and the willingness to work at it.

But that goes for most things in life.

1.6. How to use this book

This book can be read from cover to cover.

It's structured to give you:
1. A solid understanding of brand psychology.
2. A clear process for brand building.
3. A practical toolset to:
    a. *Strategize* how your brand can be valuable.
    b. *Design* the identity that communicates this value.
    c. *Build* a powerful Brand Experience.

But you don't have to follow the rules.

You can use this book as a reference guide, reading only the chapters you need for study or work assignments.

The busiest readers can just read the summary of each chapter.

The text also contains the icon ⊘. Click on it to find a worksheet, website or app that makes your job easier.

Print readers find this list of tools at www.brandbuilding.com/tools.

Downloads are free to use for your own brand.[2]

Then, a note on notes. This is not an academic book, but I did include some endnotes in case you want to call bullsh*t on anything.

"I'm calling it!"

Finally, a word on my tone. I'm far more pleasant in person than in writing.

On paper, I casually slander a lot of politically vulnerable groups like stockphoto lawyers, dead philosophers and dirty cows.

I assure you: the irreverence is of good nature.

Not *that* kind of irreverance.

However, if you happen to be offended throughout, please refer to the immortal words of Gunnery Sergeant Hartman:

The more you hate me, the more you will learn.

"You will not laugh! You will not cry!
You will learn by the numbers! I will teach you!"

All right, I see you are trembling with excitement.

We're ready to take the bull by the horns.

Let's build you a brand.

2. The Brand Building Process

2.1. Introduction

You don't want to read this part.

Creatives politely nod when planning (let alone 'Process") is mentioned and then get right on with the business of building stuff.

I'm just as stubborn. For years I started building without a process.

I skipped to the fun part, thinking I knew what people wanted and what design language they understood.

After weeks of work, I would march triumphant, grinning like a possum eating a sweet tater. I believed I had built yet another masterpiece. Sadly:

Without a plan, I ended up redoing most of the work.

That proud feeling just before reality sets in.

Winging it never works. Your audience *needs* a consistent message.

This is not achieved by improvising your way through your branding materials. You need to approach brand building like a professional and think it through.

A methodical approach can seem stifling. But creativity without structure is like fuel without an engine. It burns brightly but doesn't get you very far.

And unless you're a celebrated modern artist, no-one will appreciate your chaotic mess.

"This brand is called: A Wilderness of Desire"

A process also helps to get your team on board. A brand has to be carried by the entire organization, and:

Rallying around a common process helps build support.

Lone riders have to force their team into cooperation.

"Where's my f&%#ing logo, Steve?"

And unless you're running a gulag, that might not be the way to go. So:

A process provides structure and support for your brand.

A brand must sing in unison.

Luckily, I've build you one.

2.2. The Brand Building Pyramid™

The picture below explains how we're going to do things.

First, we learn the basics of changing minds with brand psychology.

Then, we build a brand. This is done in 3 stages:

1. *Strategize* how and for whom your brand is useful.
2. *Design* the identity that communicates this usefulness.
3. *Build* a convincing Brand Experience.

I will walk you through each of these in the following chapters.

Go to www.brandbuilding.com for tools 🔧 to ease your journey.

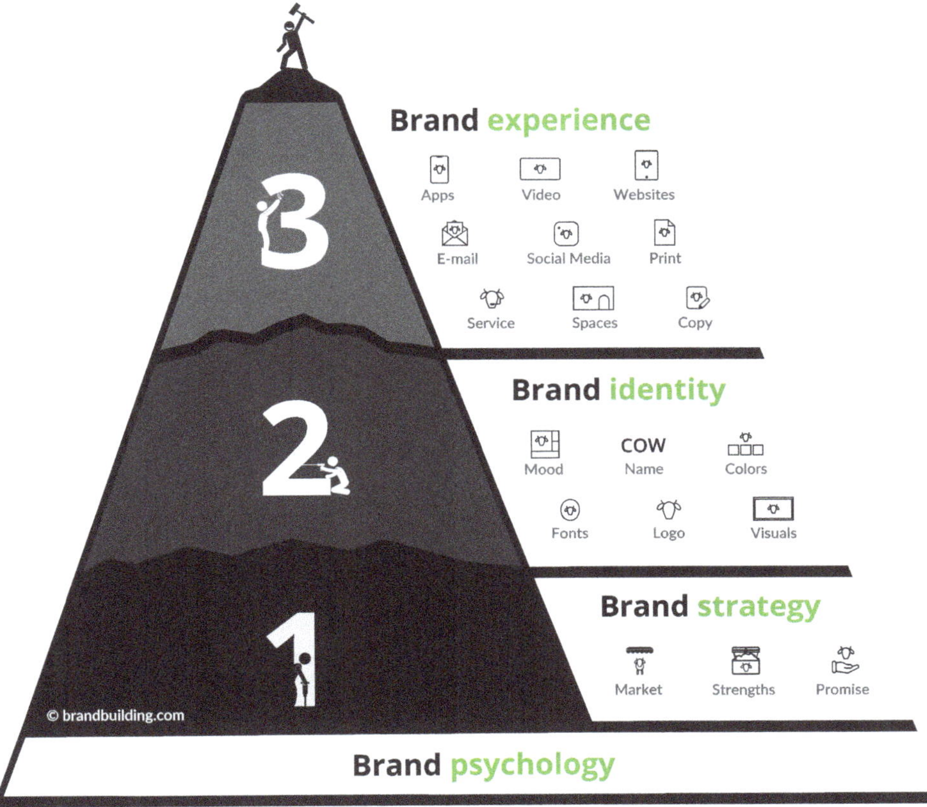

2.3. Why you should test your choices

"The only true wisdom is in knowing you know nothing."

Socrates

You're about to build a brand. Now, most brand builders consider themselves artists. This is a problem, because:

Artists don't test the assumptions underneath their work.

They hate contaminating their art with rigid thought. And of course. Because who wants their creative vision sullied?

Yet you are more like a mason.

What you are.

What you are not.

Because as you build your brand, you are confronted with some choices:

Do we target segment A or B? (Brand Strategy)

Do we paint our product red or green? (Brand Identity)

Do we hide the menu on our website's landing pages? (Brand Experience)

To make each choice you need assumptions.

Based on your assumptions, you choose segment A, a green product and landing pages without menus.

Your assumptions might be true. But they also might not be.

For even a demi-god with broad experience and great ability (thank you) is not all-knowing.

"Sorry guys, even I test stuff."

You - however - don't even represent your average customer. This means your assumptions might be (1) slightly off or (2) flat-out wrong. Now danger lurks, for:

Bad choices are built on bad assumptions.

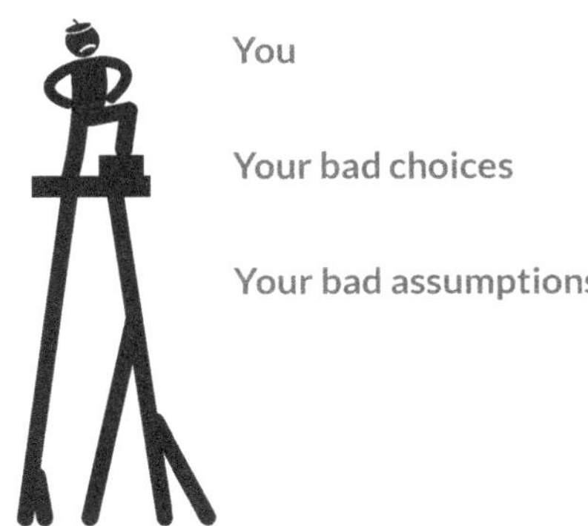

Since bad choices come with frustration, career damage and/or debt, we want to avoid them if possible.

So assume only this: You know nothing.

Don't assume segment A is better. You don't know.

Don't assume people prefer green. You don't know.

Don't assume landing pages without menus convert better. You don't know.

Socrates and his philosopher buddies agreed that to "think you are wise when you are not"[3] is an obstacle to knowledge, because:

No-one seeks to know what he thinks he already knows.

So assume nothing. Test each assumption along the way.

This can seem like more work. But it isn't. Because you spend less time re-doing things.

Yet there's a painful price to testing assumptions. You risk your ego. Your ideas might be proven wrong, and that hurts.

Now your ego will always seduce you to go with your gut. And why not? You are brilliant. Why not just roll with it? You can always rework it later?

"Nah bro. We don't need to test stuff.
Let's build something awesome!"

Yet the only alternative to testing assumptions is trial-and-error.

You build a brand, the market refuses it, you try a different brand.

This can be very labor-intensive. Especially if your mistakes concern Brand Strategy, the fundament underneath your other efforts.

After all, you can easily rework a landing page, but choosing a new market segment? You'll have to start over.

"... but it burns... so brightly!"

You see: trial-and-error is not suited for defining Brand Strategy or Brand Identity.

However, you can experiment with pieces of your Brand Experience. There, we even have a name for it: A/B testing. (More on that later.)

So keep that ego in check. Test your assumptions. Measure like a mason.

Then how should you go about this? Great question.

The Brand Building Pyramid's steps each come with their own testing methods. I will discuss them in the following chapters.

Use them to build a solid Brand Strategy, Identity, and Experience.

Probe absolutely everything.

Don't bother with market research firms.

They do not ask the questions that matter.

Instead, they produce mountains of irrelevant data and analysis. Why? Because the fools hiring them interpret glut as hard work.

"Here. Now strategize."

Only let other people handle your market research if you (1) have excess money, (2) could use a pawn to sacrifice if your brand fails or (3) need fuel for that fireplace in your beach house.

For now, I'll assume none of these apply. So instead, start with what growth hackers call "rapid experimentation" and rigorously test every element of your brand.

As the American engineer Edwards Deming said:

"In God we trust. All others must bring data."

2.4. How to test Brand Strategy

"The truth is never told during the nine-to-five hours."

Hunter S. Thompson

In the first stage, you decide what you'll offer to whom. These decisions come with a lot of assumptions about your audience, each of which you have to test.

Offer the wrong thing to the wrong audience, and your project dies.

This is very common, and the road is littered with products, politicians, and careerists who failed to match with the market.[4]

This match is called product/market fit. Without it, a brand is useless.

No matter how strong your brand, a lack of product/market fit means your project is not useful enough to the people you're pitching to. And as we saw in the introduction, a strong brand can never redeem a useless project.

Verify assumptions on Brand Strategy by interviewing your audience.

Don't just ask your girlfriend if your idea is cool. Of course she'll say yes. Close and not so close people will always avoid hurting your ego.

Instead of criticizing your plans, they'll give you enough false positives to quit that job and ruin your life.

But even mommy liked
my guitar-as-a-service idea.

These can be 5 or 15-minute talks. Keep it casual. Locate their pains with simple questions:

- How do you solve X now?
- Why do you bother with X?
- What are the implications of X not working?
- Talk me through the last time X happened?
- Where does the money come from to solve X?
- Who else should I talk to regarding X?
- Is there anything else I should have asked?

Focus on *them* and *their* pains. These conversations are not about you. Don't tell them about your project before you've truly understood what their pains are.

When you finally tell them about your project, beware of inviting fake praise. Words like "I would definitely buy your cow", or "Sure, I'll vote for you." are meaningless.

Only real commitment signals real enthusiasm.

Real commitments are pre-orders, deposits, donations or letters of intent. But also a willingness to trial your software, volunteer for your cause or making intros to people important to you.

Invest in brand building after you are (relatively) sure about product/market fit.

Real product/market fit.

Imagined product/market fit.

This will save you a lot of disappointment. And even if your audience hates your project, consider it a win. At least you didn't splurge time and money on a brand.

So rigorously test your assumptions by interviewing your audience.

Because as Mike Pence once said:

"Enhanced interrogation saves lives."

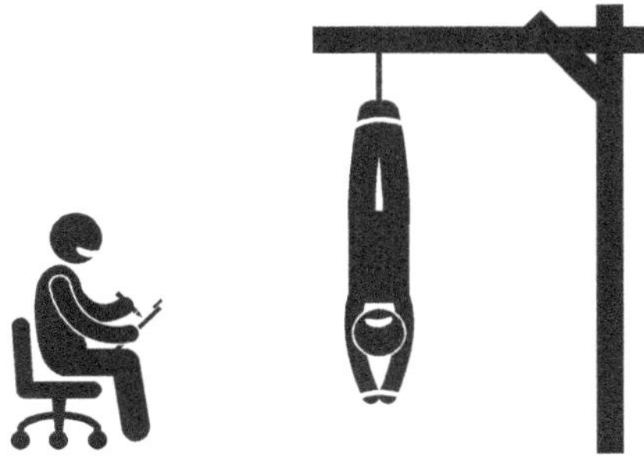

Now why don't we give us
some truthful answers?

2.5. How to test Brand Identity & Experience

"If you've got the truth you can demonstrate it. Talking doesn't prove it."

Robert A. Heinlein

Brand choices – from logos to copy – invite a lot of debate. This is healthy.

Yet debate can force team members into concessions that reduce their buy-in and enthusiasm.

Design phases

1: Brainstorm

2. Healthy discussion

3. Unhealthy discussion

4. Winners & losers

Luckily, the opinion of your audience is the only thing that really matters.

Not yours, not your bosses, and certainly not Bob's (from accounting). Therefore I recommend testing to help you make important choices.

Just ask your audience to pick a favorite option, navigate a page you build or if they understand your pitch.

You should replace debates with data by running test.

This does more than just safeguarding your physical health:
- ✓ *Be more confident* when choosing a direction with actual data.
- ✓ *Skip the nasty fights* that come with the emotional subject of our brand.
- ✓ *Promote user-centric* by making your team win over the crowd.
- ✓ *Harvest ideas* from your audience, just like from brainstorming.

2.6. How to run tests

Testing is simple if you know the steps.

Step 1: Select a tool and a panel to run your tests

You don't have to hit the streets with a clipboard. There are online tools 🔧 for testing. They collect the answers and analyze the results.

High rolling readers can buy fresh eyeballs for each questionnaire.
- ✓ Filter for age, gender and other things that represent your audience.
- ✓ You can ask the same question multiple times.
- ✓ Mercenaries are brutally honest.
- ✗ Can become expensive quickly.
- ✗ Mercenaries won't always offer quality input when asked.

Frugal readers can ask their friends or customers to answer questions.
- ✓ Free! Yay!
- ✓ Soul mates are more generous with their own input.
- ✗ Family and friends don't necessarily represent your audience.
- ✗ Soul mates go easy on the criticism.
- ✗ The results will come in slower.
- ✗ Volunteers tire. You can't keep asking them.

Step 2: Present the panel with a real choice

Setting up a test is an investment for you and your panel. Make it usefull.
- Provide real alternatives for every concept.
- Make a selection of 3 logos, not 1.
- Propose 3 headlines, not 1.

But don't offer too many, for people are most comfortable choosing if the choice is limited. This is called 'choice paralysis'.

The test audience doesn't know everything you know. Make sure what you present your audience is:

- *Relevant.* Does it send the message you want it to?
- *Distinctive.* Does it stand out amongst similar brands?
- *Memorable.* Does it evoke enough emotion to be remembered?

Step 3: Ask questions about the choice

You can ask the test audience why they chose the design they did. Besides preference, you can ask how cool, trustworthy or clear it is.

Good questions find out if your brand promise has been made:

- Which design looks the most trustworthy?
- Which design looks the easiest to use?
- What would you have done differently?

The feedback allows you to find out areas for improvement. Or merge the best parts of each tested designs plus the feedback into a hybrid.

Step 4: Make sure your results are statistically significant

Statistical significance means your design isn't beating the others by chance. If you ask just 10 people and the result is close, it's not really significant.

But your results are conclusive *and* significant, you can safely rebuff team members who still want to champion their preference.

While there's no accounting for taste, numbers never lie.

3.7. Why you need a band book

Aristotle

With brand building, every step builds on the previous ones. So every time you build a piece of your brand, it should harmonize with all your previous choices. To make this easy:

Your decisions should be collected in a brand book.

Your brand book contains your entire brand identity:
- ✓ Brand promise
- ✓ Logo and logo variations
- ✓ Colors
- ✓ Fonts
- ✓ Icons & images

A brand book keeps your brand uniform.

No cooking stuff without the brand book.

The brand book allows you to keep your troops in line and quickly brief other parties on your brand. It also allows you to show off to your investors.

Perhaps the corporate brand books you've seen inspired some cynicism. Let it go. You don't have to use the vanilla, one-size-fits-all, politically neutral prose, nor does it have to be formatted properly.

Heck, you don't even have to call it a brand book. But write down your decisions, and collect them in one place.

2.8. Summary

You are a mason, not an artist.

Test must test (any assumptions underneath) your Brand Strategy, Identity, and Experience. By testing your work, you build on the truth and not on your fancies.

Most of our ideas will turn out to be wrong.

It will hurt. But the upside is worth it. By sampling everything, we won't have our 7-course meal sent back into the kitchen.

"Perhaps some more of that brand, sir?"

You also need to structure your brand building efforts.

Collect your decisions in a brand book. For a cohesive brand, ensure every step builds on your previous work.

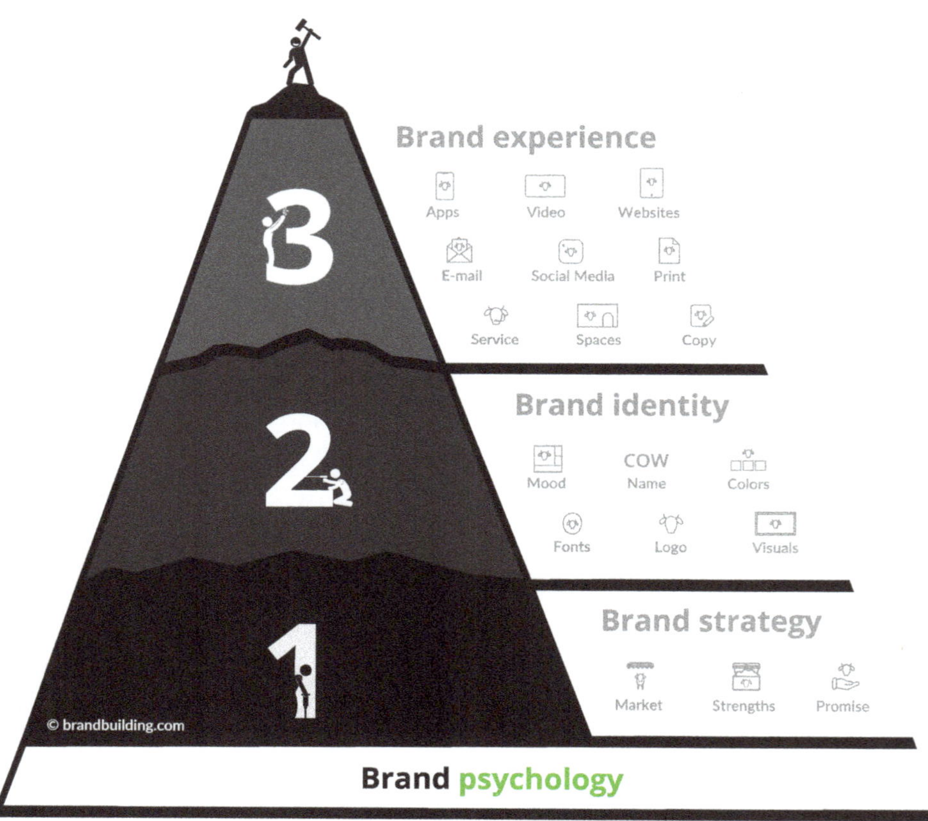

Brand experience
3
Apps
Video
Websites
E-mail
Social Media
Print
Service
Spaces
Copy
Brand identity
2
Mood
COW
Name
Colors
Fonts
Logo
Visuals
Brand strategy
1
Market
Strengths
Promise
© brandbuilding.com
Brand psychology

3. The psychology of branding

3.1 Introduction

Brands aim to influence decision making by changing minds. That's why you – the brand builder - have to know how minds work.

This isn't hard. Minds work eerily similar across cultures, genders, and ages.

They are all pliable, suggestible and prone to influence.

Just how we like them.

We all have simple minds.
That includes you.

3.2. Needs are eternal

Let's start with an innocent statistic.

We are three times as rich since the 1940s, yet our happiness didn't budge.[5] Take a look at this (simplified) graph:

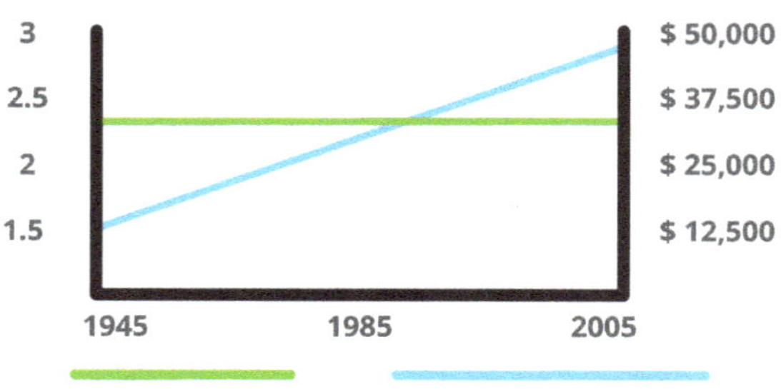

U.S. happiness v.s. Real GDP per capita

Kings couldn't dream of the luxuries we enjoy today, from air travel to Angry Birds. Yet:

We always feel like we *need* something.

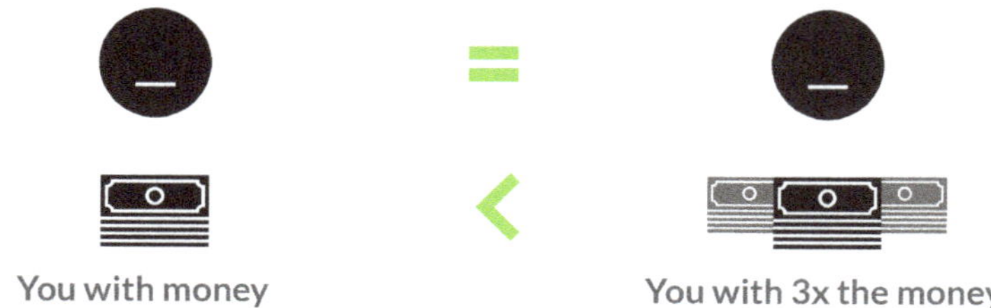

You with money

You with 3x the money

We apparently dislike being mortal and finite. (Speak for yourself, though.)

Our condition comes with many painful side effects.

Boredom. Loneliness. Illness.

But also compassion, ambition, and spirituality.

Therefore we're always open to brands who will fix these pains. This means:

There will always be a market for your project – IF it fixes someone's pain.

Fix someone's pain or be redundant.

And the stronger the pain, the more potential for your brand.

No pain.   Some pain.   Severe pain.   Extreme pain.

No customer.   Good customer.   Great customer.   No more customer.

Yes. Most pains are illusory and most consumption unnecessary. Resources are scarce and there is an island of trash in the ocean. (I mean the plastic, not England.)

"Carry on."

But this book isn't about the evils of capitalism.

It's about building brands that sell.

3.3. Emotion beats logic

Everybody thinks they're rational. Even the crazies.

We could easily fill every asylum.

But then why do we buy things we don't need? Or donate to ineffective charities? Or vote for idiots? The reason is simple:

Decision making is not rational. It is emotional.

And not just for the ill-fated in rehab. As humans, we all rely heavily on our emotions to make the simplest of decisions.

The neuroscientist Damasio discovered that damage in the part of the brain that handles emotions left his patients unable to choose between a turkey or a chicken sandwich:

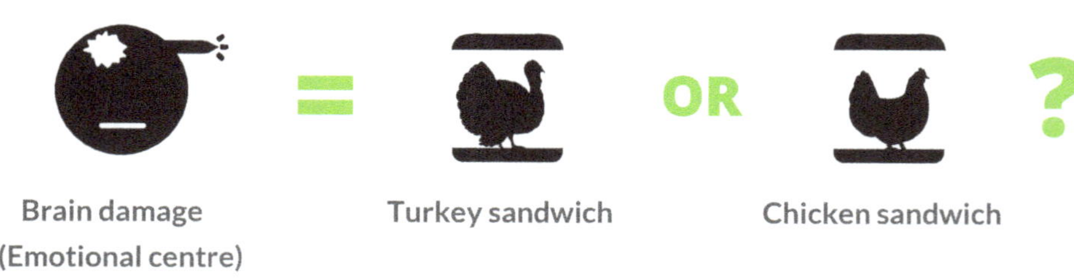

| Brain damage (Emotional centre) | Turkey sandwich | Chicken sandwich |

He argued that:

The point of choice is always based on emotion.

Effective decision making is simply impossible without the motivation and meaning that spring from emotions.

That's why you shouldn't just make a reasonable case with your brand, you must stir the right emotions in your audience.

No-one will choose your brand because their rational brain dictates it. People choose because they feel it's in their interest to do so. Remember:

Emotion beats logic. Always.

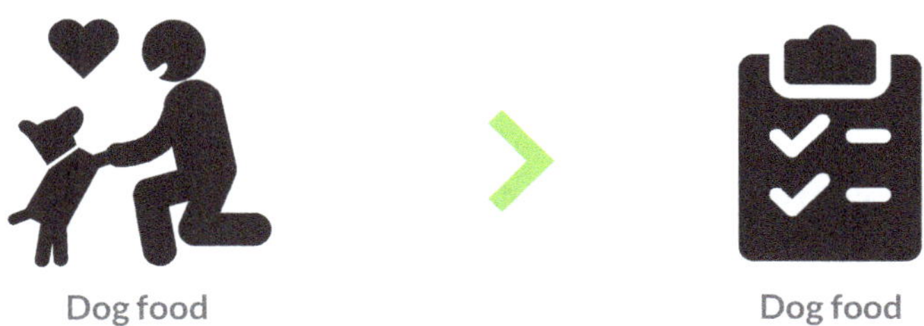

Dog food > Dog food

Consumers want to feel a sense of thrill or belonging. Donors want to feel a sense of charity or moral righteousness. Voters want to feel a sense of security or patriotism.

Everyone wants to feel right when making a decision. That's why:

Your brand should make a promise that stirs the right emotions.

That promise allows you to enter the part of your customer's brain where the decisions are made.

The rational brain will reason to justify the emotional decision.

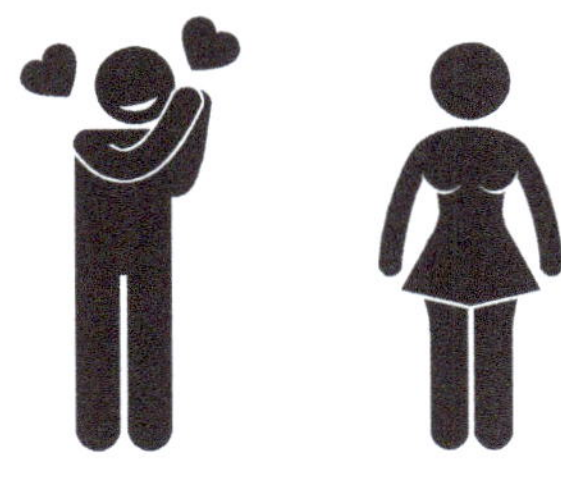
I bet she's super smart!

Let's explore these ideas further.

3.4. People judge instantly

Nowadays, the average attention span is a short as this sentence.

How about pitching this person?

Your brand is competing with the world, which includes cat videos and battle royale games. There are a billion ways to spend your time and money.

This means:

Nobody is waiting for *another* brand.

No-one will gather around the fire with you. There is simply too little time.

Don't forget, you are dealing with humans. And humans are busy.

They are swamped with work. Their stocks are tanking.

Or their wife is angry because they keep ending the hopes and dreams of countless noobs in epic Call of Duty killing sprees.

Someone shooting up the noobs.
(Not caring about your brand.)

Ahem.

People are busy and have limited headspace.

The evolutionary remedy is to speed things up. In 'Blink', Malcolm Gladwell shows us how instinct and intuition are used to quickly sift through incoming impulses.

Dealing with every project on offer is impossible. Therefore:

People judge your brand within a split second.

The brand builder shall make his case.
He is granted a split second.

This is all the time you have to convince people that your brand is worthy of attention.

If the judgment is unfavorable, your brand is discarded on the heap of annoyances.

If the judgment is favorable – and that bar is very high – your brand is given a further look.

Do not fool yourself. This rule applies to those on social media or visiting conferences. Everyone's busy. Everyone's impatient. And they are all very familiar with useless clutter in their lives.

It is your job as a brand builder to make them pay attention in that split second.

Make your brand stir the right emotion. Let your brand immediately address their needs.

Because no-one cares about your brand just because it's new. They want their pains fixed.

If you do your job right, you will be rewarded.

A powerful first impression can hook the customer.

If you manage to stand out, people will invest some of their attention to explore what's on offer.

3.5. Pictures are powerful

We saw you (1) have a split second to (2) stir a positive emotion.

How are you going to crack this puzzle? Perhaps our ancestors held the key when they painted stick figures on the walls of their stone cribs. They reasoned that:

A picture says more than a thousand words.

Advertising hunting services.

We know this to be intuitively true.

Because we all prefer pictures to reading.

But pictures – beyond their convenience – pack a powerful punch. They have more impact than words have. Shakespeare himself would admit that - for all the beauty of words:

Pictures make a lasting impression.

Your mind can instantly conjure up that Baywatch poster of your youth. The paper has long withered since, but the memory hasn't.

This picture doesn't do her justice.
But we have a brand to adhere to.

A picture did what a 1,000-word description of a woman in a bathing suit could never do:

Pictures help us remember.

Can you recall the story your colleague told you at lunch? Or the plot of the last novel you read?

Exactly.

But don't feel bad: Your brain is just not wired for it. Studies show that people remember just 10% of what they hear, 20% of what they read, but 80% of what they see and do.

What do you remember from your last holiday?

Furthermore:

Pictures save time.

No matter your reading level, it's always faster to look at something than to read about it. Some even claim that visuals are processed 60.000x faster than text.

Reading about the renaissance. Looking at Michelangelo's David.

Often:

Pictures convey complex ideas with a single image.

Paintings portray a life story. Movie posters sketch the setting or even the plot. A few icons convey important psychological mechanisms.

Given the time frame that you have to arouse interest, you must become adept at using pictures. Because in the service of your brand:

Pictures help communicate value.

We defined *value* as the extent to which people *perceive* your project as useful. And for this *perception*, she often relies heavily on the pictures.

Your brand images have to look good.

They need to evoke the right emotion.

But above all, they must portray something valuable..

3.6. Trust is key

Why did the UBS bank issue a 44-page manual to their staff on how to dress and smell, forbidding them to eat garlic or wear 'gaudy sunglasses'?

They answered this question themselves after it leaked: "[We aim] to impress customers with a *polished presence* and a sense of Swiss precision." (Emphasis mine)

Translation: we want to be taken seriously. And they are right.

Would you:

Entrust your money to man with garlic breath and gaudy sunglasses?

Donate to a charity of which the directors drive luxury cars?

Vote for a politician who 'evolved' her stance on your favorite issue?

If we see something off, we think the project must be off.

My wife says that for every rat you see, there are 20 you don't see.

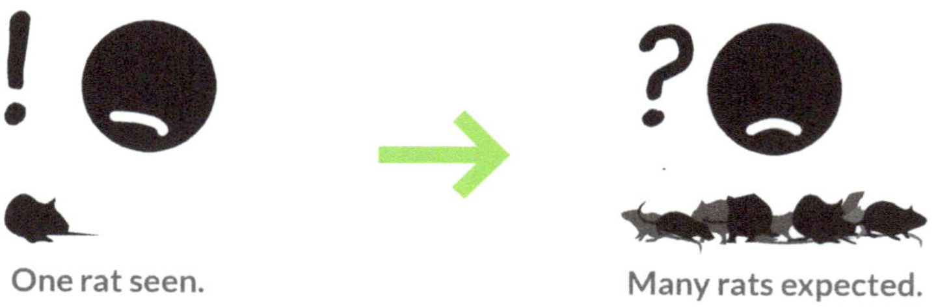

One rat seen.

Many rats expected.

People see a rat and they cringe. Then they wonder what else is wrong.

Something suddenly doesn't feel right and their rational brain will start arguing.

However:

People won't tell you they don't trust your brand.

Instead, they moan about a time that is "inconvenient", a price that is "unrealistic" or they are not "comfortable" voting for a candidate.

That's why every element of your brand is important and you should minimize faults.

If your brand contains faults, trust is breached. And without trust, there is no transaction, no donation, no vote. In other words:

Trust is the key to a commitment to your project.

You can't blame folks for protecting themselves. Everyone has been burned at least once. So have you. Because every market contains clowns and criminals peddling hogwash.

How about some hogwash?

In short, you need trust for a commitment to your brand.

So polish your brand until it contains the minimum amount of faults.

And never - ever - wear gaudy sunglasses.

3.7. People mirror their peers

My grandfather was a prudent saver. He slowly became affluent, yet remained afraid to buy his dream car.

"What would the neighbors think?", he warned himself.

Who wouldn't dare buy a 1973 Volkswagen Sirocco, you wonder? It turns out that we are wired to consider the neighbors.

When our ancestors roamed the forest in bands of hunters, it was important to be a good member of the tribe. Surviving alone in this hostile environment was impossible.

Exclusion meant death.

Aaah, the good'ol days...

Even though the pressures of finding food and shelter have waned, the intense desire to belong remains.

This need to belong can overrule reason.

The psychologist Solomon Asch proved this in his famous conformity experiments. Test subjects were told they were doing a visual perception test and asked the following:

Does A, B or C match X?

Easy enough, right?

What made it hard was that the test subject had to give the answer after a group of peers (all actors), pointed to the wrong line in unison.

Alone, only 1% gave the wrong answers. But the peer pressure resulted in:

People tend to consider their peers before committing.

Yet in every situation where you are unsure of how to behave, one often looks to others for clues.

Ambiguity makes people copy the actions of others.

This is called *social proof*.

Social proof comes in *public compliance* (despite believing the herd is wrong) but also as *private acceptance* (a belief that a herd must be correct).[6]

People just assume the herd has more information.

This is why referrals and online reviews are powerful instruments for your brand. (And according to Nielsen's Trust in Advertising studies, the most powerful.)

It is also why the long-time unemployed find it difficult to find work. Employers reason that many others already found them unemployable.

The larger the herd, the more powerful the social proof.

"If it wasn't valuable these
other f&*#ers wouldn't be here."

In what is called the 'multiple sources' effect, a larger herd is assumed to be more right than a smaller one.[7]

It is why brands buy social media followers. It boosts their credibility. If a large chunk of the herd follows the brand, it must be worth following.

The more uncertainty, the more powerful the social proof.

People are more sensitive to social proof when your brand is new to them, making a commitment risky.[8]

Therefore, when building a new brand, finding forms of social proof should be of prime importance. It lends your project credibility in the eyes of the ambiguous buyer.

Here are the 8 types of social proof:

- **Customers**: social proof from your existing customers or users (Testimonials on Trustpilot or handcrafted case studies).
- **Experts** - credible and esteemed experts in your field. (Professor X at the University of Y teaches with brandbuilding.com)
- **Celebrities** - or other influencers (That singer showcasing your product on their feed, or a photo in your restaurant).
- **Crowds** – social proof large numbers of people ("100,000+ brand builders bought this book!").
- **Friends** – people who are friends of your users/website visitors ("12 of your friends like BrandBuilding.com").
- **Certifications** – an industry-relevant institute certifies that you are an expert, high-quality or trustworthy source ("ISO certified.").
- **Press** - Prominent publications mention you. ("As seen on Famous News Site")
- **Partners** – industry leaders help realize your project. ("Proud partner of Big Company")

Showcase every bit of social proof you can muster, wherever this is appropriate.

Positive social proof greatly influences the trust in your brand. Of course, it cuts both ways. Negative social proof makes the herd distrust it.

This is why your reputation (what others think and say about you) is part of your brand.

- ✔ A good reputation enhances trust and facilitates commitment.
- ✘ A bad reputation destroys trust and prohibits commitment.

So invest in your reputation.

With positive social proof, people more easily commit to a new brand.

3.8. People satisfice

Imagine you're at a restaurant with your love interest. There are candles, perhaps some Vivaldi.

"I prefer my Vivaldi a little less personal."

The waiter appears to announce the wines on offer. He cocks an eyebrow and pouts his mouth as he opens the cabinet. Three bottles (but no prices) are revealed:

Côte-de-Brouilly   Wild Pig   Le Bert

Sadly, you're a savage who only drinks beer. Yet the waiter and your date are awaiting a decision. You can feel your cheeks burn, and a cold sweat is crawling upwards towards your neck. What bottle will you pick?

The old school claims that – confronted with a pro blem – you will gather information, identify the possible solutions, and choose the best option.

Yet there are multiple problems at your table right now:
1. As a savage, you have *limited information.*
2. People are waiting. You experience *time pressure.*
3. Unsure if you want a cheap or a good wine, you have *vague goals.*
4. The meals haven't been chosen yet. They produce *changing conditions.*
5. You can't Google the wines. There are *social expectations.*

It's the same with most decisions. People browsing solutions for their needs can suffer from one or more of the above. Therefore:

People tend to satisfice. That means choosing the first reasonable option.

Naturally, people tend to satisfice more in situations where:
- They like a gamble. (You might pick a really memorable bottle.)
- The cost of a 'wrong' choice is low. (Your fine physique will close out the night anyway.)
- Weighing options does not improve your chances. (It's probably all good or all bad, given the quality of the restaurant.)

Let's get back to your date. What bottle did you choose?

And what was your need when choosing the bottle?

- To make an impression? Then you probably went for the Côte-de-Brouilly. Most readers associate its look with age, quality, and tradition.
- To save some money? Then you probably choose the Wild Pig. The simple label reminds readers of bottom-shelf supermarket offerings.
- To go risk-free? Then you probably choose the Le Bert. The bottle ticks all the boxes a decent wine should.

But no matter your need, you were forced to satisfice. That meant choosing the first reasonable option, depending on your need. And in doing so, you relied on the label – the brand - to make your choice.

3.9. Value depends on context

The waiter returns with the expensive Côte-de-Brouilly. With a playful look, you mention the price tag and gesture to your date that (s)he better taste the wine. There is a giggle as the waiter arches his back in a perfect 15 degrees whilst pouring the dollop.

While the waiter expounding on its origins there is a twirl of the glass... a noseful of aroma... the sip...

Your date is impressed!

Of course she is.

The price influences her judgment.

And she is not alone. Test subjects judge wine tastier if it has a high price, even though given the exact same 'cheap' wine seconds before.[9]

The price tag changes how the brain fires. It makes the wine *seem* tastier.

The take-away?

Context changes how your project is experienced.

This goes for all bodily sensations.

Researchers had people judge the quality of a product standing on soft carpets and hard floors. The comfy carpet made them judge more favorably.[10]

Now before you dismiss these folks as fools, let me tell you another story.

When Bordeaux University asked 50 professional wine tasters to describe a white wine dyed red, they used jargon typically reserved for red wine!

Sights, sounds, and smells change minds.

Environmental factors change how we interpret reality. It changes our attitudes and beliefs.

That's why supermarkets make sure you can smell their bakery. Why sauna's spray eucalyptus around. And why you shouldn't sh*t before selling your home.

Right. In short:

The context influences how people experience value.

So don't be shy when determining your price. A big price is interpreted as big value.

Be sure the context in which you present your project feels, looks, sounds and smells right.

And always choose the expensive bottle. Your date will like the taste.

3.10. Authority helps

In the famous Milgram experiment, you get to torture someone to death because an authority figure told you so.

A hidden actor answers your questions, and with each wrong answer, you can administer an electric shock. It gets stronger over time, finally allowing you to deliver deadly doses over his agonizing screams.

You'd walk out, right? Good for you. Because 60% 'kills' the actor because the guy in charge of the experiment tells them to continue.

He is the experimenter.
It is all right.

How is this sadistic anecdote relevant?

Well, there are countless ways to borrow authority for your brand, allowing you to invoke the same reasoning in your buyers:

When experts say something is all right, it probably is, even if it does not seem so.

For example, take skincare brand reps. They wear lab coats, giving them an air of authority. They tell you what your skin 'needs' and what you 'have to do' each morning.

She wears a lab coat.
It is all right.

Or how about the sports hero advertising shoes, telling you to 'just do it'? Surely the $250 investment enables you to dominate a stadium like him?

He is acclaimed.
It is all right.

Sometimes, it's just random. Like singers endorsing a charity or a political figure, proclaiming 'it is the right thing to do'.

She is always on TV.
It is all right.

Perhaps you can blow some budget on celebrity. But most likely you'll have to get creative if you want some authority for your brand.

So why not start with lab coats?

3.11. Be likable

The more you like a person, the easier they can persuade you.

This might sound self-evident, but hear me out. Because what makes someone like a brand?

First off, be like your audience.

In the words of the science fiction writer Asimov:

"All things being equal, you root for your own sex, your own culture, your own locality… and what you want to prove is that you are better than the other person. Whomever you root for represents you. And when he wins, you win."

So when building your brand, make sure you reflect your typical customer.

Write in the tone-of-voice that matches the reader's.

If a product is made in their country, let them know.

And use models that are aspirational to them. Avoid stock photos with cardboard people if possible.

This feels awesome.

Everyone will be more comfortable if they recognize themselves in your brand.

Second, be authentic.

Many brands forget that they're selling to humans.

Our goal is to enthusiastically fashion innovative and value-added user communities to provide solutions for our partners. [11]

Ever read this? Such mission statements – when vomited up by salaried peasants – are not inspirational. Not now, not ever.

Me and someone pitching
a mission statement.

Never Disneyfie your existence. Make sure you're authentic. This goes for your entire Brand Experience.

Often, there's some room for humor. (Unless you're selling Hellfire missiles.) It breaks the tension and makes people like you.

Can be funny

Not funny

Never funny

Third, give a sh*t.

You can also be intensely personal. Selling dog food, we took every opportunity to name you and your dog, preferably in handwriting.

Shower the first fans of your brand with love, and they will certainly repay you. In the words of the entrepreneur Paul Graham:

"Take extraordinary measures not just to acquire users, but also to make them happy."

Shower them with love

Now the moment you get some traction, a little devil may suggest that your users are just hogs for the roast.

Countless businesses and politicians are seduced by this lie. Their initial success makes them feel untouchable, and this conviction leaks into their speech and actions.

Eventually, your hogs pick up on their status, and they will hate you for it. Perhaps they won't leave you immediately (because they're locked in somehow). But they will jump ship as soon as there is an alternative.

Succesful someone

His loyal customer

Keep investing in your Brand Experience if you want lasting success. Don't slack because you want to make an extra buck.

3.12. Simulate scarcity

Because when something is in short supply, you want it more.

3.13. Simplicity wins

When I wrote papers in college, I made everything sound smart.

"People are hungry" became "The body politic is regularly prone to experience a prominent esurience for sustenance."

"Money is important" became "The wealth as encapsulated into fiat currencies should be considered paramount to functioning economic entities."

I stuffed every sentence with thoughts until they mutated into literary tumors, formatted as paragraphs.

The professors loved it. They gave me lavish grades.

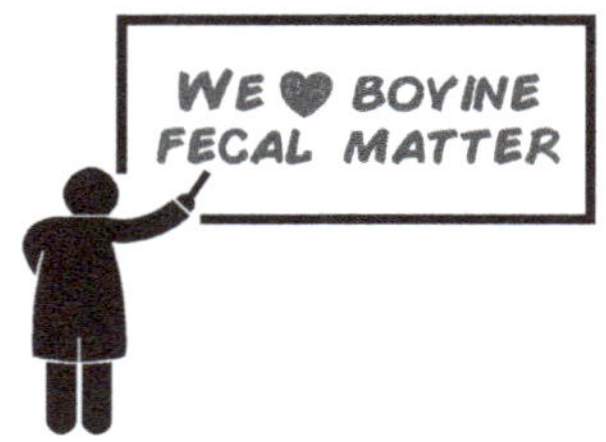

The upside down of academia

In academia, you thrive if no-one understands you.

This, however, doesn't fly in the real world. The average person has:
- Little headspace
- Little intelligence
- Little patience
- Little knowledge
- Little time
- All of the above (Most likely)

That's why:

People only digest simple thoughts.

Folks ignore everything that needs thinking.

They have enough thoughts as it is.

Every thought just adds to the pile.

This includes the PhD's reviewing my papers. No-one read them. They were glossed over and *perceived* as intelligent.

And I don't blame them.

Thinking is a costly investment with uncertain returns.

So, when building a brand, you need to simplify.

✓ Strip things that shouldn't be in focus.
✓ Eliminate jargon.
✓ Shorten your sentences.
✓ Decrease the number of syllables.
✓ Visualize important ideas.

Simplify, simplify, simplify. Until a 12-year old can understand it.

Will this good-for-nothing 12-year-old
understand your brand?

In branding, you thrive if everyone understands you.

It doesn't matter if you're selling dog food to house wives, or aircraft to specialists. Be crystal clear about how your project solves their pain.

Did you ever have to explain Netflix to your parents? Of course not. It's the simplest brand around. Netflix is useful because it's immediately understood by everyone.

Your brand should be easy to understand, easy to commit to, and easy to use.

Siegel+Gale ranks brands according to this simplicity.[12] They prove that:

Simple brands outperform brands that are perceived as more complex.

No wonder. We saw that people require a positive emotion to commit to something. But if you pitch them something complex, how much positive emotion remains? And if using it is difficult, how loyal will they be?

He won't be buying.

Radically simplify your brand.

In business:

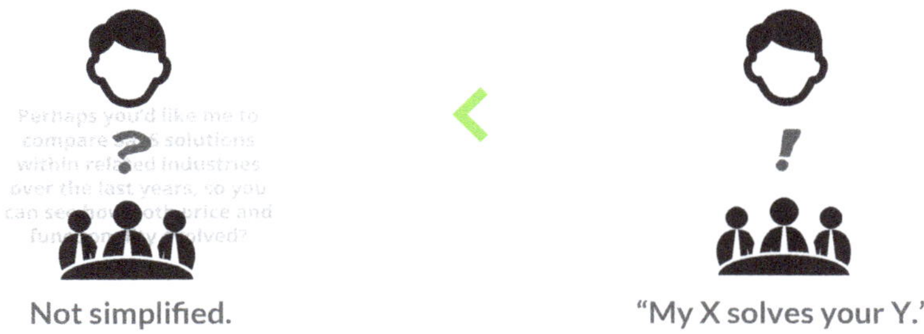

As in politics:

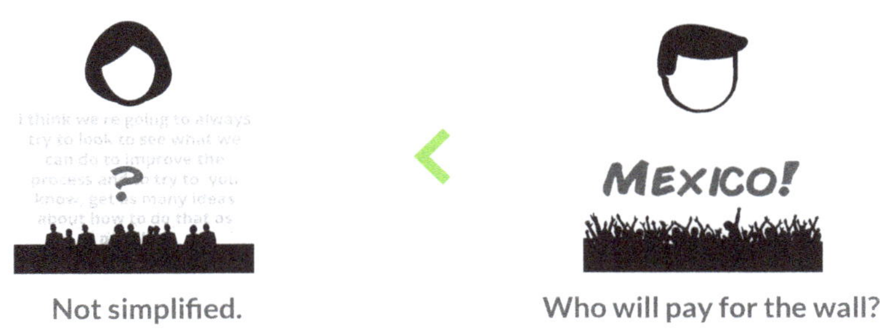

If your audience is thinking, you've failed.

Simplicity is an art in itself. If you want to convince your audience, you need to practice it with zeal. As Albert Einstein said:

"Everything should be made as simple as possible, but not simpler."

3.14. Summary

In this chapter, I told you some facts about brand psychology.

Some of these can seem Machiavellian.

But this is the marketplace.

It's brutal and unforgiving in weeding out the weak.

So there is no use for edifying talk on how these facts shouldn't be.

Because they are and have been since your ancestors crawled out of the sea to trade seashells for sex.

Do you take seashells?

Use these facts when building your brand. Neglect them at your peril.

Don't concern yourself with the hypothetical customers who judge your project on its merits only. They don't exist.

And even if you find a unicorn willing to commit to your sh*tstained brand, she will only be good for one transaction.

So, eat the truth.

Then decide to bring the strongest possible brand to your market.

It's the only way to win.

In the following chapters, we'll build you a brand to mimic the success of the greatest businesses and shrewdest politicians. It will tell the right story to the right audience in the right way.

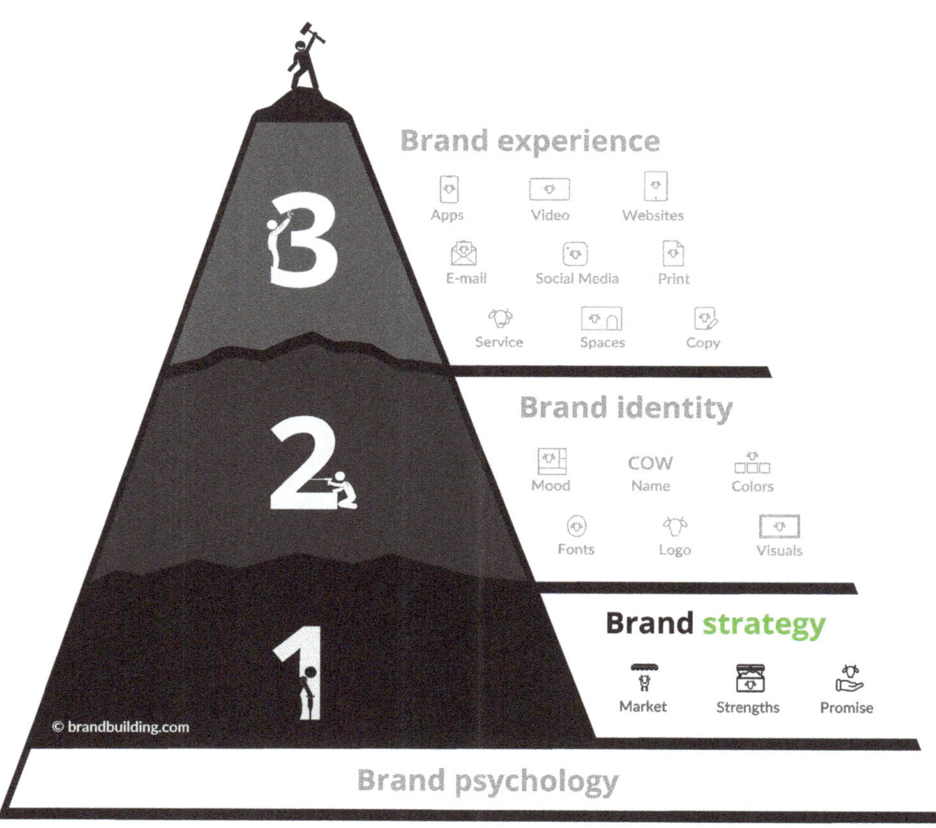

Brand experience
Apps
Video
Websites
E-mail
Social Media
Print
Service
Spaces
Copy
3
Brand identity
Mood
COW
Name
Colors
Fonts
Logo
Visuals
2
Brand strategy
Market
Strengths
Promise
1
© brandbuilding.com
Brand psychology

4. Brand Strategy (Stage 1)

4.1. Introduction

"Strategy 101 is about choices: You can't be all things to all people."

Michael Porter

If you don't know where you're going, any road can take you there. With these immortal (and paraphrased) words did the Cheshire Cat send Alice on her way.

The same goes for building your brand. If you don't know what you are going to promise to who, it doesn't matter how it's presented.

You've got this.

Think about your project and your market before you start building.

You can't just dabble away and expect to come up with a great result that will inspire customer loyalty, blow the competition out of the water and crown you the king of commerce.

To the contrary.

Without a strategy, you will tell the wrong story to the wrong people.

I learned this lesson the hard way.

Our new recycling shower was a miracle. We sold it from every angle:

He ain't buying no shower.

Exhausted yet? You are not alone. People politely listened to our drivel, then turned away to indefinitely "think about it". And I don't blame them.

Our brand was mosaic. It juggled multiple messages. It felt inconsistent. Besides, those who we spoke to weren't into buying them. Needless to say, we didn't sell many showers.

Sadly, this problem is very common. Luckily, the solution is simple:

Strategize. Then decide what to promise to whom.

Don't roll your eyes at me just yet. I'm not talking about high-brow PowerPoints delivered by well-groomed frats from elite universities. That kind of strategy is useless. (Unless you're force-feeding change to minions.)

"Kill... me..."

And apart from the well-groomed frat thing, that's not me. So relax. I won't use stuffy words or complex graphs.

I'll keep it extremely practical and extremely simple.

4.2. How to analyse the market

"Know and understand the customer so well the [brand] fits him and sells itself."
Michael Porter

In the good ole' days, you could stumble out of your hamlet, grab a cow from the barn and tread a dusty path to the market. You were the only cow trader in town, so your competition was limited to other delicacies like hogs and chickens.

But the modern marketplace is noisy and crowded. There are thousands of vendors, from every part of the world, each bellowing from the top of their lungs.

It is impossible to sell something without either (1) slashing your price, (2) murdering the competition, or (3) positioning your brand as something uniquely useful.

Slash your price.

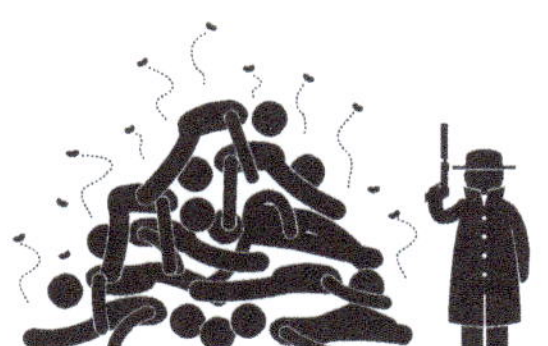

Murder the competition.

Be uniquely useful.

Since you won't make a dime on the first option and the second poses some legal hurdles, this book focusses on option three:

Make the market think your project is uniquely useful.

Now what is useful to one isn't useful to others. In a market, some are looking for milk, others for meat. Consequently:

You need to find out which customers have which needs.

For this chapter, I recommend using the Brand Strategy Worksheet ⊘ at www.brandbuilding.com

Step 1: Describe your customer segments

We start with a very basic question: who will think your project is useful?

Most likely you have a pretty good idea who that might be. You could be selling an exotic glue useful to a tiny group of stamp collectors. Or perhaps your new soda should be consumed by everyone, from Fifth Avenue to the Kalahari Bush.

Whatever it might be, it pays to be explicit and specific when you are identifying your potential audiences. Even if everyone needs your stuff, you can identify who will be most likely to be your best customers. It will help you focus.

So who needs your project? Can you identify them and put a line around them, grouping them in 'customer segments'? What is their age, gender, interests? How do they spend money? What else is relevant?

Write it all down. At minimum, list:

A. List their needs, or even better, their pains.

These can be hard needs like price, quality, convenience, etc. Or soft needs: recognition, status, emotional, etc.

B. List their personalities, attitudes, and values.

Include demographics like age, sex, location, income, occupation, education, industry.

Then go one step further with psychographics. Write down interests, lifestyle, behavior, opinions, and values.

C. List the channels they use to reach competitors.

Do they shop online or offline in brick-and-mortar stores? Are they using intermediaries to buy similar stuff?

When you are done, you should have a list of segments. Here's an oversimplified example:

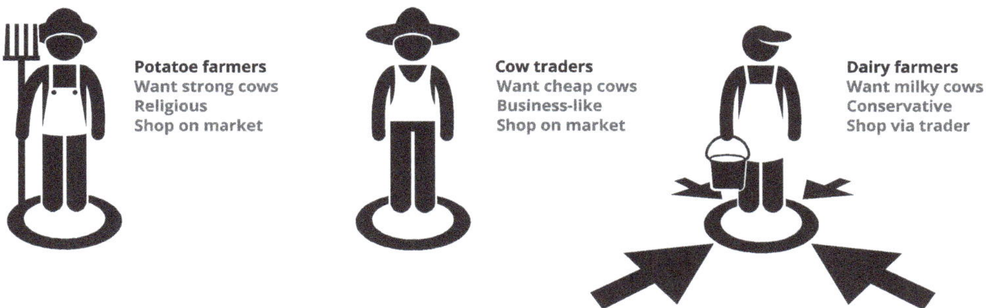

D. Fill the top-left quadrant of the Brand Strategy Canvas. (Optional)

Step 2: Describe your competitors

Next, find out what your competitors are offering these segments. Be sure to include your indirect competition. These are vendors who sell different products, but which fulfill the same need. The reason beer manufacturers lobbied against the legalization of weed is that they basically serve the same need: getting wasted.

A. What unique usefulness do your competitors claim?

What is their reason for being - their unique selling point? What else is good about them? Can you find them everywhere? Do they have great service? Perhaps they're very cheap.

B. What needs do they leave unaddressed?

Are there any things they don't offer? Perhaps they are leaving money on the table by selling a dry product without a strong brand that offers extra status? Or perhaps the status is all they offer, and the product can be much improved? What are their shortcomings?

C. Which (sub)segments are they serving?

Who are they delivering to? And why them? Is there big volume or big margin to be captured there? Can you identify segment they don't serve?

What are competitors offering your segments?

You now have analyzed the market by listing the relevant segments and competitive offerings. You already smell opportunity! In the next chapter, we will see if you got what it takes to conquer a segment.

D. Fill the bottom-left quadrant of the Brand Strategy Canvas. (Optional)

Summary and steps for analyzing the market

The market is crowded. You can only make money by offering something that is uniquely useful to the right audience. You can discover what your brand should promise by analyzing the market.

- ☑ **Step 1: Describe your customer segments:**
    - A. List their needs, or even better, their pains.
    - B. List their personalities, attitudes, and values.
    - C. List the channels they use to reach competitors.
    - D. Fill the top-left quadrant of the Brand Strategy Canvas. (Optional)
- ☑ **Step 2: Describe your (indirect) competitors:**
    - A. What do they promise?
    - B. Where do they fall short?
    - C. What segments do they serve and how?
    - D. Fill the bottom-left quadrant of the Brand Strategy Canvas. (Optional)

4.4. How to consider of your strengths

"Every skill you acquire doubles your odds of success."

Scott Adams

You probably suspect someone is craving for your project. And that there's a juicy piece of market waiting for your triumphant arrival.

Or perhaps the market is saturated with vendors and all the segments are served. Then you must dislodge a slacking competitor with a superior offering.

In any case, it is time to consider your strengths.

For this chapter, I recommend using the Brand Strategy Worksheet ⊘ at www.brandbuilding.com

Step 1: Find out what makes your organization unique

We all have desirable traits, as individuals and organizations. These traits come in handy when executing on the opportunities you're smelling.

A. Write down what your organization is good at.

Maybe you have a lot of money or a great network of partners. Perhaps it's unique expertise or a number of patents.

Also write down the things that you stand for, the things you want your brand to breathe. Commonly called 'values', some examples are:

Easygoing
We do things
informally

Reliable
We leave only
happy customers

Innovative
We're always on
the cutting edge

B. Write down what your organization stands for.

You now have a list of things that make you unique. But perhaps it isn't enough.

Often, organizations don't have all the resources they need. The talent, money, network or internal drive required to conquer new segments just isn't there.

Or perhaps you yourself lack the brains, bucks, buddies or balls to chase your dreams

The ultimate entrepreneur
(With balls being a metaphor)

Finding the resources to exploit opportunity is a chicken-egg problem.

The egg comes first, dumbass.
You can't just have a chicken.

Without the success, you don't have the resource to generate success.

But there is a solution. You can stack your resources until you have a combination that – taken together – is unique.

The cartoonist Scott Adams describes his 'talent stack' as follows:

I don't have much artistic talent, and I've never taken a writing class. But few people are good at both drawing and writing. When you add in my ordinary business skills, my strong work ethic, my risk tolerance, and my reasonably good sense of humor, I'm fairly unique. And in this case, that **uniqueness** *has commercial value. (Emphasis mine)*

You can combine seemingly ordinary resources to become extraordinary.

If you lack a skill, you can learn it to set yourself apart from others. This can take time, but every extra skill opens up more opportunities.

C. Describe how your strengths and values mix to make you unique.

Organizations can fill some gaps where necessary, but often not all gaps. Focus on how to become extraordinary enough for the opportunity ahead.

D. Fill the top-right quadrant of the Brand Strategy Canvas. (Optional)

Step 2: List the ways in which your project is useful

The project you are branding has some obvious qualities.

A. Write down the tangible benefits of your project.

But usefulness goes beyond what your project does.

For example, you don't just buy a car because it has good mileage. It's about *how it makes you feel* and *who you are* when you drive your BMW to your jealous friends.

You don't just vote for a politician because she supports or opposes gay marriage. It's about *who you are* as a liberal or conservative.

It's why designer clothes are uniquely useful. They are not uniquely durable or insulating. But they can communicate to others that you're successful and should be respected.

This should do the trick.

Positive emotions and identities are as useful as tangible benefits.

B. Write down the intangible benefits and identities of your project.

Now, most projects offer many benefits. However, not all of them are useful in themselves. But often, like with resources, you can combine benefits that stack up to something useful.

C. Describe how the (in)tangible benefits combine into something unique.

Remember, you must be able to offer something uniquely useful. Failing this, you will end up competing on price, not making any money.

D. Fill the top-right quadrant of the Brand Strategy Canvas. (Optional)

Summary and steps for considering your strengths

To take advantage of opportunities in the market, both your organization and your project have to be uniquely useful.

☑ **Step 1: Find out what makes your organization unique:**
  A. List your strengths.
  B. Write down your values.
  C. Describe how your strengths and values mix to make you unique.
  D. Fill the top-right quadrant of the Brand Strategy Canvas. (Optional)
☑ **Step 2: List the ways in which your project is useful:**
  A. Write down the tangible benefits of your project.
  B. Write down the intangible benefits and identities of your project.
  C. Describe how your (in)tangible benefits work together to make your project unique.
  D. Fill the bottom-right quadrant of the Brand Strategy Canvas. (Optional)

4.5. How to make a brand promise

"People do not buy goods and services. They buy relations, stories, and magic."

Seth Godin

Now it's time for the final step. We choose what to promise whom.

Your brand promise is a claim of unique usefulness to your segment.

If you get it right, your audience will choose your brand over the competitors. They'll give their time, money or vote to you.

Before making the promise, we will consider:
- The needs of your market segment(s).
- The promises of the competition.
- What makes you(r organization) unique.
- What makes your project unique.

For this chapter, I recommend using the Brand Strategy Worksheet 🔧 at www.brandbuilding.com

Step 1: Choose your segment(s)

You have divided the market into segments and described each of them. Perhaps more than one segment seems attractive. And the more segments you serve, the bigger the potential reach of your brand. But:

You can't be all things to all people.

The more specific your segment(s), the more tailored your message will be and the bigger the chance it resonates.

Specific customer segment	Multiple customer segments
Tailored message	Uniform message
Narrow appeal	Broad appeal
Feels intimate	Feels distant
Easy to conquer territory	Hard to conquer territory

This doesn't mean that your tailored brand won't have wide appeal.

Tailored brands can be picked up by the masses once a trend-setting segment has adopted it.

That's why Paypal targetted eBay's top sellers, and luxury brands mobilize celebreties.

Step 2: Highlight a project benefit

We saw that your project offers many benefits. But which benefit matters most to your chosen segment?

The answer is simple. We focus on the main quality that your segment is looking for. If they are hungry, offer meat. If they are thirsty, offer milk. And don't forget the intangibles you are offering like status or guilt relief. In other words:

Focus on the pain of your segment.

- Selling makeup to teenagers? Focus on the pain of not belonging and promise acceptance.
- Selling hardware to gamers? Focus on the pain of losing and promise an edge in competition.
- Selling cappuchino's in a hip city? Focus on the pain of solitude and promise an authentic experience.

By focussing on the pain, you instantly get your customers' attention. Why? Because they've been struggling, and perhaps actively looking for a solution. Pains include the need for status, community, or authenticity.

Pick the (intangible) benefit(s) you think will resonate most.

Don't pack too many benefits in your promise:
- ✘ No-one will believe you.
- ✘ You don't have the time to communicate multiple unique benefits.
- ✘ No-one will remember multiple unique benefits.

The more benefits you stress, the less clear and powerful your promise.

Step 3: Dodge the competition

Your competitors are already making promises. If they offer similar promises, you can one-up them by offering a superior one. Or, you can find a hole and fill it by serving a fresh promise to an ignored segment.

The more unique your promise, the easier to conquer your segment.

If your brand enters a crowded market, others might already claim similar uniqueness. This means your territory is taken.

Since every crowded market has a leader and a bunch of also-rans, it allows you to see clearly which promises are not being made and which segments are underserved.

In a busy market, make sure your promise is truly unique.

"That was my line!"

Never do the thing that too many others in the market are trying to do.If you find that some competitors are very dominant, perhaps you can focus on an underserved segment. Look for the hole – and then fill it.

The more common your promise, the harder it is to capture attention.

But perhaps you get there first and the market is nearly empty. You can then establish a leadership position by making your promise to the audience first.

You have the added uniqueness of being the first, so make sure to communicate this.

Pioneers can claim leadership by being the first.

But you can only remain the leader by being the best. If a competitor arrives with a superior promise to the same segment, they will quickly dispose of you despite you being first.

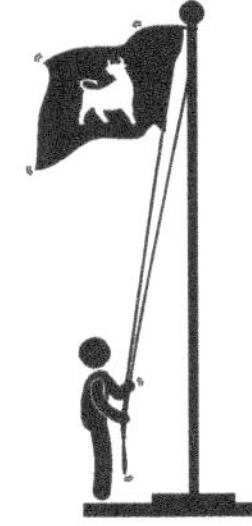

We were the first.
We are the best.

Step 4: Make sure you're credible and competent.

Finally, you need to make sure you are credible enough to make the promise, and good enough to execute on it.

Lavish promises require great credibility.

A common attack in presidential politics is that candidates "lack experience". The implicit suggestion is that the candidate's promises will never be fulfilled because he or she isn't credible enough.

In business, it is also important to be seen as a credible player. Anything beyond a lemonade stand requires significant skills, and the bigger your promise the larger your credibility has to be.

Especially when your innovation produces a leap over existing solutions, making the old way of doing things redundant. In this scenario, your promise sounds messianic and the competition will preach your inevitable demise.

Lavish promises require great execution power.

As we discussed in the introduction, you actually have to fulfill the promises you make if you want to avoid severe damage to your brand's reputation. So make sure that you are capable to fill the hole in the market you're eying.

If your talents match the challenge, you can make the promise.

But be very honest in your assessment. Making promises is easier than delivering on them. If you require more resources to fulfill these promises, this should be made explicit.

If you want to avoid embarrassment and reputational damage at all cost, always follow the old adage: "underpromise, overdeliver."

Step 5. Turn your promise into a war cry.

Now you have a clear picture of who (organization) will promise what (project benefit) to whom (segment), and why it's superior (from competitors).

- Buy my cow for delicious milk.
- Subscribe to my dog food service for a healthy dog.
- Vote for me to keep the foreigners out and bring manufacturing back.

But this doesn't sound very sexy. It won't inspire your audience, nor your own troops.

Your brand promise has to bring out a (strong) positive emotion.

Because in that busy marketplace, with a glimmer of contact between you and your potential buyer, what will you yell at him to stop him in his tracks? How will you convince busy people to consider your cow in that split second?

You need to convert your ordinary promise into a memorable war cry.

In my town, there is a market with a successful trader. He spends his time behind some rickety tables covered with plastic sheets and strawberries. When you arrive on any given Saturday, you can hear his booming voice from afar. Now, what do you think this veteran salesman is yelling?

✖ *"Buy my strawberries, they are nice and cheap!"*

or,

✖ *"Buy these Spanish imports, they are delicious and affordable!"*

Of course not. He knows that addressing the pain of those in his market bluntly is useless. They need low-cost fruit, for the supermarket is too expensive. That's why they are here.

Yet they also want to avoid the slack that you make soap with. In short, their need is fruit of affordable quality.

But our salesman doesn't address this need directly, for his crowd doesn't want to be reminded of their poverty. At best, he fails to inspire. At worst, he insults. So he takes a playful line that he can use for 8 hours straight:

Now let's dissect this ingenious war cry:
- ✓ *"Juicy"* is a powerful word that conveys not only quality but also a taste experience. Saliva runs down your cheeks merely hearing it.
- ✓ *"3 for 2"* signals a deal can be made. It's affordable, but not overtly so.
- ✓ By focussing on strawberries only, he keeps his proposition simple and asks little of your attention.
- ✓ His bare inventory has you assume he's a strawberry specialist.

Now let's look at a brand promise for those that won't visit a peasant market until a nuclear holocaust forces them too.

"I have new needs now."

Most people have used anti-dandruff shampoo in their lives. Imagine making a brand promise to teenagers like this:

"Don't be a social outcast! Remove dandruff with our chemical shampoo!"

This wouldn't work. This approach addresses the pain rudely directly, and fails to evoke a positive emotion, something we saw was crucial for decision making. Hence they say:

"Be hug ready."

Like this, they force you to *visualize a situation* where their project has addressed your pain. They also make you cringe. For if you don't buy their product, you'll be clutching people's faces to your dandruff-riddled shoulders. Yuck.

The promise should indirectly address the need and visualize a positive end result.

Now imagine me selling customized dog food to middle-aged women whose dogs are often overweight. We take out a billboard and scream:

"Fix that obese embarrassment of a dog. Buy our customized dog food!"

That'd be a bit rough. So let's say:

"Keep your best friend healthy and fit."

The promise should evoke a positive emotion.

Here we communicate several things.
- It's not your fault the dog is fat. She just requires tailor-made food.
- It's your best friend so don't be stingy.
- It keeps her healthy and fit. Better not unsubscribe.
- Healthy and fit are practically synonyms. Yet I plant the visual of a vital dog doing nature stuff.

Every syllable adds meaning to a promise. Weigh them well.

An effective war cry is crucial for your brand's success. Some pointers:

- ✓ Be inspired. See how your favorite brands do it.
- ✓ Be bold. Water it down to appeal to everyone makes it appeal to no one.
- ✓ Be visual. Try to conjure the ideal situation after fixing the pain.
- ✓ Be brief. Use as little words as possible.
- ✓ Be simple. Assume the cognitive abilities of a 12-year old.
- ✓ Be tactful. Don't address someone's pain directly. It's sensitive.
- ✓ Be sharp. Strong consonants like K, C, T pierce the brain. Make America Great Again beat Stronger Together.
- ✓ Be prolific. Write down as many as you can. Don't settle for the first.
- ✓ Be scientific. Test what works best.
- ✓ Be poetic. Use rhyme, alliteration, double-entendres, repetition or reversals to make the message stick.

Brand	Promise	War cry
Coca-Cola	Buy our caffeinated soda for a savory energy boost.	Open happiness.
Volvo	Buy our durable cars to keep your family safe.	For life.
Head & Shoulders	Buy our chemical shampoo to remove your dandruff.	Be hug ready.
M&M's	Buy our sugar-coated chocolate for a tasty treat.	Melts in your mouth, not in your hands.
U.S. Marine Corps	Join our ranks to earn the respect of your country.	The few. The proud. The Marines.
De Beers Group	Buy a diamond to show that your love is eternal.	A diamond is forever.
Solar Monkey	Subscribe to our software for easy solar designs.	Solar sales simplified.
Toby	Subscribe to our dog food service for tailored food.	Keep your best friend healthy and fit.

Summary and steps for making a brand promise

You need to make a brand promise. This is a claim of unique usefulness to your segment. Get it right and your audience will choose your brand over the competitors.

- ☑ Step 1: Choose your segment(s).
- ☑ Step 2: Highlight a project benefit. Focus on unserved pain.
- ☑ Step 3: Dodge the competition.
    - I. Crowded market? Make sure your promise is unique.
    - II. Empty market? Claim to be the first and the best.
- ☑ Step 4: Make sure you're credible and competent.
- ☑ Step 5. Turn your promise into a war cry.

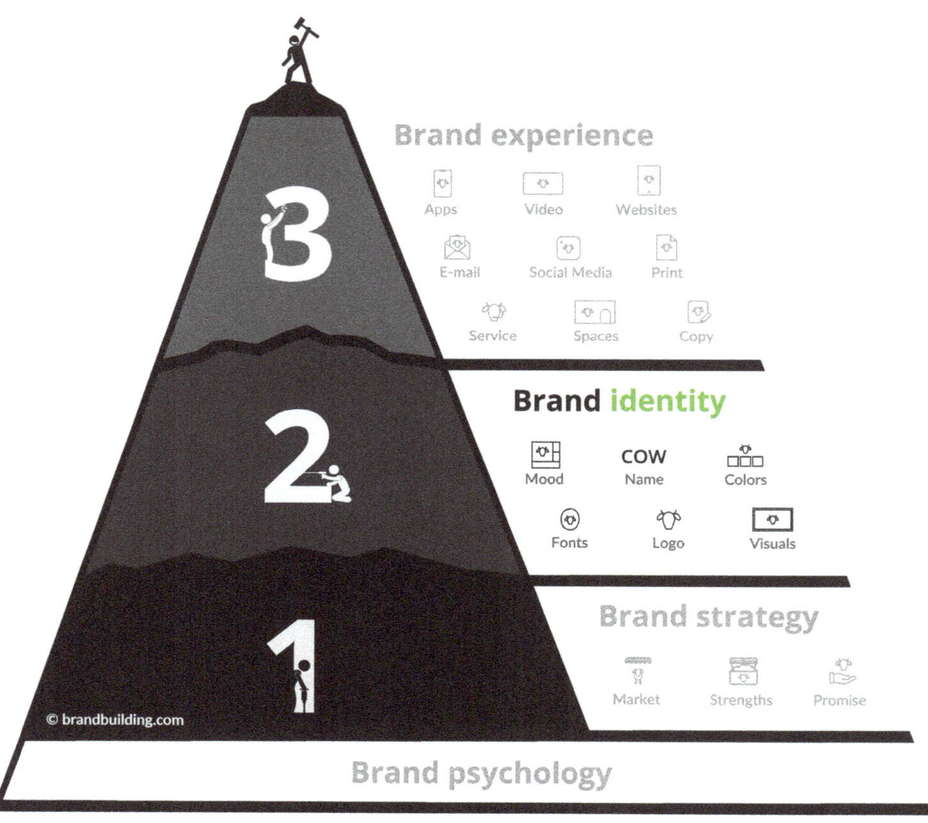
Brand experience
3
Apps
Video
Websites
E-mail
Social Media
Print
Service
Spaces
Copy
Brand identity
2
Mood
COW
Name
Colors
Fonts
Logo
Visuals
Brand strategy
1
Market
Strengths
Promise
© brandbuilding.com
Brand psychology

5. Brand Identity (Stage 2)

5.1. Introduction

"Design is the silent ambassador of your brand."

Paul Rand

You now have a firm foundation to build on. With your brand promise in hand, it is time to design the basic building blocks of your brand, the identity. These are the mood, name, colors, fonts, logo, and images.

Brand Identity contains the building blocks for Brand Experience.

These building blocks show up everywhere in your Brand Experience, so its strengths and weaknesses will boost or haunt you everywhere.

It's also not easy to revisit these choices. If you later decide to recolor your logo or change a font, you'll have to mutate your entire Brand Experience – from website to brochures.

At the end of each chapter, I offer a summary, steps and some tips on where to store your work. These keep your project organized.

Most chapters have tools 🔧 to help you out. Click on the icon or go to www.brandbuilding.com

5.2. How to make a mood board

"The principles of true art is not to portray, but to evoke."

Jerzy Kosiński

You know what your brand must promise. But the transition from words to images is very hard. Even the literary gifted (thank you) use visuals to clarify their ideas.

"So that's a cow!"

Luckily, there is a simple method to migrate your strategic thinking from the realm of imagination to something concrete. It's called a mood board.

Mood boards visualize your brand promise.

In essence, mood boards are collages of images you will find online and offline. It can contain cut-outs of magazines, photos of packaging you liked or the greeting card your granny send you.

Besides sketching the "mood" your brand should evoke, they provide inspiration for the fonts, images, illustrations, colors, and logos that you're about to develop.

This chapter covers:
- ✓ Rules for mood boards.
- ✓ Steps for making and presenting a mood board.

Rules for mood boards

Even though no-one outside your organization will see your mood board, there are many advantages to making one.

Use mood boards to build consensus.

A mood board is a great opportunity to involve your team or client – if you are designing an identity for someone else.

You can build consensus on what the brand should look like and which feelings it should evoke. These discussions will be far easier to have now.

Because once Brand Identity elements – colors, logo's, etc. - they often feel wrong to colleagues or clients, without them able to articulate why.

A mood board settles everyone on a direction before the real work starts. And everyone who was allowed real-estate on the mood board tends to buy into the project.

Build multiple mood boards.

The choice offered by two or three concepts will make the resolve for a direction even firmer. It's more work, but moods are best judged in context.

They're also a political instrument. Bad ideas can be stashed on one mood board which is then voted down. This allows you to shepherd your vision without disrespecting those who still have to buy in.

Choose to make physical or digital moodboard.

If you're old-school, you can collect your clippings and prints in a shoebox, then buy an empty foamboard and paste your inspiration onto it.

However, since physical mood boards are hard to reorganize and share, I prefer using Pinterest ⬤ to collect my inspiration. It allows you organize inspiration neatly in one place.

Designers have many abilities, but very few are psychic. So, if you're hiring one for designing your Brand Identity, brief her with both your strategic thinking and a mood board.

"Wow! Do you also do therapy?"

Step 1: Collect the ingredients

The Michaelangelo's amongst my readers will be knee-deep in cut-outs by now. For the brainy types, I've compiled a list of ingredients for your board:

✓ **Images** – The bread and butter of your board. Add all the photos, illustrations, posters and advertisements that hint at the proper feeling. Then dig a bit deeper. What images are related to your originals?

✓ **Colors** – What colors define your brand? Will you be a warm brand – selling soda? Or a cool brand – selling lab equipment? Are you loud with bold colors or discreet with muted colors?

✓ **Metaphors** – Perhaps your organization is very sustainable or artisan. Are there visual metaphors that evoke this? Like a polar bear or a chisel? And how about your project qualities? If it's healing, you might want to include a fresh garden or a fountain. If it contains a fighting spirit, you might want to use lions. Stay away from metaphors with bad connotations like hyenas, communists or Canadians.

✓ **Quotes** – Are there any sayings from famous people that capture the spirit of your brand? Recruiting agencies always plaster their walls with aspirational quotes. Be careful not to ruin your mood board with corny platitudes.

✓ **Textures** – Paper, fabric, glass or wood, all are uniquely textured and can bring a special touch to your brand. This is handy if you deal in physical things or have a physical store to decorate.

✓ **Fonts –** You will settle on fonts in a later chapter. Yet perhaps there is some calligraphy that instantly evokes the mood you are looking for.

Every item should evoke and visualize your brand promise.

Step 2: Curate and organize your ingredients

Mood boards can be whatever works for you – from orderly outlines to crazy collages. But before you start pasting together random thoughts like a serial killer – let's review the rules.

"It's about minimalism, you see now?"

The mood board should convey the brand promise to your audience.

This is not about you and your fancies, it's about what appeals to your chosen segment. What grabs their interest and attention? Your mood board should focus on what conveys the brand promise to your audience.

The mood board should be consistent.

The board doesn't have to be a modern-art masterpiece. But only a consistent whole can provide visual guidance in a direction. Don't include logos or pictures just because they tickle you funny.

Calibrate the volume.

If you clog your mood board with every relevant image, it will cause sensory overload and confuse everyone. However, just a few images won't provide adequate inspiration and direction. Therefore, keep a nice mean between a lot and a little.

Step 3: Fancify your mood board (optional).

Are you presenting to your boss or a client? Insert your collected content in a moodboard template 🔧. and rock their socks off.

For extra effect, print the designed mood board on a foam board and leave it behind after presenting.

Summary and steps for making a mood board

Mood boards visualize your brand promise. They give direction by converting words into images.

- ☑ Step 1: Collect the ingredients that evoke/visualize the brand promise.
    - I. Use Pinterest
    - II. Use an empty shoebox.
- ☑ Step 2: Curate and organize your materials
- ☑ Step 3: Fancify (optional).

Save your work in a folder called "/brandname/identity/mood-boards/". Take screenshots of your Pinterest board or photos of your physical mood board.

5.3. How to choose a great brand name

"I've got the hottest brand in the world."

Donald Trump

There is a reason cows are named Betty-312 and the like. Because nobody gives a damn. They are just one of many in the field. But since you want to stand out, you need a name that enables everyone to identify, remember, discuss and compare your brand.

Your brand name is the most important part of your identity.

Where a good name gets a brand accepted in the marketplace, a bad name will curse it. So be critical and don't settle until you are absolutely happy.

In this chapter, we'll cover the steps for settling on a great name. You can download a worksheet for your brand name at www.brandbuilding.com.

You can use this chapter for both your organization and individual projects.

Step 1: Brainstorm for brand names

Brainstorming is easier said than done. You'll also need constraints to be creative, so settle on these first:

- What is your brand promise?
- What kind of mood should the name evoke?
- What kind of mood should the name avoid?

Then take these constraints and start working within them.

- Which words can serve as ingredients?
- Can you abbreviate them or use their syllables?
- Are there synonyms or plays-on-words that you can use?
- Can you remove or add a letter? (Flickr, Fiverr)
- Are the names of the founders useable? (Rothschild)
- Can you use the business that you are in? (Southwest Airlines)
- Is there an experience or image you can use? (Hotjar)
- Can you take a regular word? (Apple)
- How about an acronym? (NASA)

Got a few names? Well done.

Step 2: Check which brand names are good

To avoid an emotional debate over preferences, it helps to have a neutral checklist. Are your names:

- ✔ **Distinctive** - Does your name stand out in a busy market place? Or can it be easily confused with regular, everyday words? Don't be boring.
- ✔ **Easy** - Is it short enough to be remembered? In my experience, two syllables are best. You will want people to say the whole brand name when they mention you. Also, try to avoid using unorthodox spelling or make it hard to wrap your tongue around. Don't be a mouth full.

- ✓ **Appropriate -** Is there a fit with your project/organization? Does it carry the connotations that you want it to carry? Don't be random.
- ✓ **Likable -** Does it roll off your tongue like the word "Croissant"? (Using the pretentious French pronunciation.) Will people enjoy speaking the name and telling their friends about you? Don't be unsexy.

Did some pass the checklist? Great. You've now got a list of good names. Let's find out if you can use them.

Step 3: Check which brand names are available

You must verify if your brand name or a similar one is taken.

A. First, Google the name and see what pops up.

A similar brand might be using the name. Or perhaps you find another reason to not use it. We were about to call our dog-food business "Dogler" when we discovered this was a meme for dogs looking like Hitler. Don't believe me? Google it yourself.

Make sure nothing evils pops up
when you Google the name

B. Use a tool ⊘ to check if it the name is already trademarked.

Similar names can result in someone mistaking your brand for another. This will get you in trouble, as the owner of the name will cease-and-desist you to protect his brand.

Don't piss off the rightful owners

If there is any doubt, you can apply for a trademark and hope the owner doesn't object within the time limit. When a fuss is made, you can then refer to your established rights.

But when venturing into grey territory, always consult a legal person. He will tell you what all conservative professionals will tell you: better don't.

Yet the cowboys amongst you might try. If your competitor neither has a war chest nor a legion of lawyers, you might get your way.

Taking a shootout versus someone unarmed...

C. Check if the .com name is still available.

Use a tool 🧭 to check if the .com name is still available.

Probably not, since the majority of letter/number combinations are taken, as well as the entire dictionary. But if you've been creative enough, you'll have a chance.

Naturally, you can use different extensions like .net and .org, or the more hip .app and .io.

But the .com gives your brand a lot more authority. You can always buy a domain, as I did for toby.nl and brandbuilding.com. Often, this costs thousands of dollars, even after brisk negotiation. So always evaluate if the authority and brand power you gain is worth the money.

Theoretically, it is possible to displace 'domain squatters' in certain jurisdictions, but this can be a costly and uncertain legal fight. I recommend you spend your energy on building a brand.

D. Check for availability on the social media channels you plan to use.

If your domain or social media handles are unavailable, this should be taken into consideration when choosing a name. Check online 🔧.

However, it doesn't have to stop you. You can try adding prefixes to the brand name until you hit a word that is available across all the channels:

Toby > gotoby.com, trytoby.com, mytoby.com, etc.

Step 4: Check which names are preferred by your segment.

You've now got a list of good and available names. You should see which one is liked most by your segment.

Relax, you don't have to hit the streets with a clipboard. You can use a tool 🔧 to do a simple online poll.

But have people sort out your good and available names by preference. The more they represent your chosen segment(s), the more weight should be attributed to their preference.

Step 5: Choose and register your brand name.

Use a domain service to book the domain name and claim the social media handles. You can also apply for a trademark 🔧, but this will cost money.

Summary and steps for choosing a brand name

This chapter covers the steps for settling on a great name for your organization or individual products/projects.

Your brand name is the most important part of your identity. You can use the worksheet at www.brandbuilding.com/tools.

- ☑ Step 1: Brainstorm for brand names.
- ☑ Step 2: Are the names distinctive, easy, appropriate and likable?
- ☑ Step 3: Check for availability:
    - A. What pops up when you search for it?
    - B. Is the name or a similar sounding name registered?
    - C. Is the .com or other relevant domain available?
    - D. Are your social media platforms available?
- ☑ Step 4: Choose your favorite names and test with your segment.
- ☑ Step 5: Choose and claim your name.

Name your root folder after your chosen name: "/brandname/"

5.4. How to choose the right brand colors

"At every era of his existence and his history, the human being has associated color with his joys, his actions, and his pleasures."

Fernand Léger

From your office décor to your business cards, colors communicate very strong messages about your brand.

You can make or break perceptions with the right or wrong brand colors.

Your audience makes an initial judgment of a brand within the first moments of interaction. At least 50% of that judgment is based on color.[13]

In fact, color is so important to branding that you can protect specific hues with copyright law.

So let's choose you the right brand colors.

This chapter covers:
- ✓ The psychology of color.
- ✓ Personal preference vs general rules.
- ✓ Steps for creating a color palette.

The psychology of color

Colors evoke strong emotions in your audience. This happens in the deepest part of our brain. We cannot shut off their effects, and most of them happen without our conscious consent. In other words:

The effects of color on your audience are largely automatic.

In Drunk Tank Pink, author Adam Alter describes how the police paint their holding cells a certain hue of pink in order to calm delinquents down.

"I guess I could be more nurturing..."

He also mentions a football team dying the opponent's dressing room in the same pink, attempting to pacify their competitive instincts before a game.

"I feel weirdly vulnerable today..."

Colors directly influence behavior.

Hot-colored pills (red, orange) work better as stimulants whilst cool-colored pills (blue, green) work better as depressants. This dramatic effect is seen in all human activity.

Red

Passion, Love, Boldness,
Excitement, Fire.

Aggression, War,
Revolution, Anger.

Green

Health, Wealth, Fertility,
Growth, Sustainability.

Jealousy, Illness, Greed
Envy, Corruption.

Yellow

Joy, Intellect,
Optimism, Warmth.

Hazard, Depression
Deceit, Cowardice.

White

Purity, Perfection,
Hope, Light, Peace.

Empty.

Blue

Knowledge, Trustworthiness,
Calm, Professional, Efficient.

Cold, Aloof.

Pink

Femininity, Caring,
Nurturing, Sympathy.

Weak, Inhibited.

Purple

Royalty, Wisdom,
Imagination, Quality.

Arrogant, Gaudy,
Profane, Inferior.

Brown

Stable, Rugged, Natural
Tradition, Reliable

Dirty, Dull,
Poverty.

Grey

Elegance, Neutral
Respect, Simplicity.

Decay, Pollution,
Damp, Bland.

Orange

Creativity, Uniqueness,
Energy, Happiness.

Emotional, Frustration,
Flamboyant.

Black

Luxury, Glamour, Security,
Sophistication, Expensive.

Fear, Secrecy, Mourning,
Oppressive, Heavy.

Branding is no exception.

So what colors should you use? Well, It all depends on your brand promise. Do you want your brand to be seen as expensive or affordable? Rough or sophisticated? Exciting or reliable?

If your brand fulfills a need or solves a problem, you might go for blue or green. But if you want to signal social status or some cool attitude, you might use black or orange.

Colors should evoke the brand promise.

That's why McDonald's changed from red to green. And why the riot police drops the blue for black when the sh*t hits the fan.

Beastmode is better in black.

Your hamburger tastes less toxic when the logo is green. And you feel more intimidated by black-clad enforcers.

If the brand colors do not match the brand promise, you're in trouble.

No one would buy brown lingerie, for brown means rugged. Likewise, pink outdoors gear would only be sold to genderqueer hunters. (A very small market, or so I'm told.)

Ze sure looks hot in hir pink gear!

Every color shades into others.

This means that if you choose a color between blue and green, you will carry associations from both, albeit muddled.

Personal preference vs general rules

Different people have different reactions to colors. Some think grey is cool. Others think it's dull. That's why your phone is sold in pink and gold for the ladies and black and grey for the men, making sure everyone is served.

You can use different colors to serve personal preferences.

Yet certain rules hold across genders and cultures:
- Most people like blue.
- Most people dislike yellow.
- Brown is hard to pull off.
- Bright colors are remembered more easily.
- Primary colors (red, yellow, blue) are remembered more easily.

Keep these in the back of your mind as you pick your colors. But don't let them guide your thinking too much: focus on what your brand has to promise.

It's time to pick some colors for your brand.

A. Choose one or two main colors that evoke your brand promise.

You can use a visual on your mood board. There are tools ⚙ to distill colors from them. Alternatively, you can use a palette collection ⚙ for inspiration.

B. Limit your main colors to PANTONE colors.

Pantone is a company that defined the proprietary colors used in printing. If you pick one of their colors, you're sure it can be reproduced everywhere.

I strongly advise using the PANTONE color picker, ⚙ instead of using regular color coding like RGB, CMYK or HEX.

PANTONE colors allow for full-color consistency across your entire Brand Experience because they can always be printed. If you're not using PANTONE, check if your colors are printable.

C. Choose multiple colors to form a harmonious palette.

Your brand needs multiple colors. While logos often use a single color, the rest of your brand requires a pallet. You can highlight different aspects with different colors.

Experiment with a color picker ⚙ to discover different shades of your chosen colors.

A palette must contain similar hues in order to maintain harmony. For example, blue and light blue are natural allies. Also:
- Some color pairs are hard to rhyme, like blue and red.
- Highly contrasting colors are experienced as disharmonious.
- Color is most easily varied across lightness (adding white).

You can make a color lighter or brighter. Tweak them to your needs.

D. Write down the codes of each color.

PANTONE, RGB, CMYK and HEX code for every color in your palette. These will be used by every graphic designer and web builder who works on your brand.

Step 2: Name your colors

The name of your color matters. You are far more likely to buy a "charcoal" colored phone than a regular "black" one. You perceive a "rose" towel as softer than the identical "red" version.

People prefer fancy color names to generic ones.

So never sell a brown cow or a red cow. Sell a "mocha" cow or a "fuschia" cow. Some lipsticks like "moonlight" or "tenderheart" don't even suggest a real hue! This step is simple: drum up something fancy and your audience thinks it's extra special.

There's no reason to say "white" when you can say "cotton".

"Autumn was more expensive.
But totally worth it."

Step 3: Test your colors

You might want to review your color selection after you've designed some more brand identity elements.

Colors are easier to judge when tangible, like in a logo or a website. By showing people several variations of a color within a logo, it's easier to tell you what they prefer. It is very hard to ask people for an opinion by just showing them a colored square.

If they think another color better expresses your brand promise, build a new palette.

Summary and steps for choosing colors for your brand.

You can make or break perceptions with the right or wrong brand colors. The effects of color on your audience are largely automatic, as they directly influence behavior.

- ☑ Step 1: Create a color palette
    - A. Choose one or two main colors that evoke your brand promise.
    - B. Limit your main colors to PANTONE colors.
    - C. Choose multiple colors to form a harmonious palette.
    - D. Write down the codes of each color.
- ☑ Step 2: Name your colors.
- ☑ Step 3: Test your choices by incorporating them in a design.

Save your work. Put your palette to a folder called "/brandname/identity/colors/". You can put the color names, colors and codes in a PowerPoint (.PPT) or a simple text file (.TXT).

5.5. How to design a powerful logo

*"Perfection is reached, not when there is nothing left to add,
but when there's nothing left to take away."*

Antoine de Saint-Exupery

In the old west, they'd stab a cow with a glowing piece of iron shaped in the owner's crest. The resulting scar tissue identified to whom it belonged.

You have to do the same. Don't scar your stuff. Instead, design a logo that allows people to identify your brand.

A logo combines typography (letters) and images (pictures) to into an image that represents your brand.

The logo – like the name – should be carefully considered. The entire mood of your brand should be evoked upon seeing it.

Of course, it takes time and money before your audience associates your logo with your brand. But you can speed up this process if you make the right choices.

Ideally, the logo is your brand promise, visualized.

You've got a very short time to make an impression. But a good logo can help you stand out and convey your brand promise in an instant.

In this chapter, we'll cover the steps to design a powerful logo.

Step 1: Choose a logo type

These are the 7 different logo types used by the world's brands.

I can't print famous logos without getting sued, so I'll illustrate them with fictitious examples.

Word logo

A special font with special colors, like for Google, FedEx and Coca-Cola.

Only use this style when you've got an easy, pronouncable name or if you're announcing a three ring circus.

Abstract logo

Marks with no immediately obvious meaning, like Adidas, Pepsi and BP.

It's easy to create something unique using just shapes and colors. Yet we all know you're no Picasso, so take it easy.

Pictoral logo

Uses a recognizable symbol or icon, like Apple, Twitter and the WWF.

Bonus points if this symbolizes the brand promise like Snapchat's ghost or WWF's fluffy panda bear.

Letter logo

Initials to abbreviate longer names, like HBO, NASA or CNN.

If you're just starting out, add your full brand name so your audience doesn't confuse it with a deadly disease.

Mixed logo

Insert image in text, or vica versa, like Amazon, Volkswagen and GE.

This is the easiest logo to make. It's inevitably unique, highly versatile and therefore the choice of many brands.

Mascotte logo

A character representing the brand like for Michelin, KFC and Pringles.

These cartoons create a familiar mood, regardless of your company culture. Drop the name once you're famous.

Emblem logo

Badges, seals and crests using text and symbols, like Starbucks and the NFL.

These give a traditional look. Universities and artisan businesses often use them.

Step 2: Find inspiration for your logo

You saw that in each logo variation I added an (abstract) representation of the brand promise: wildly expensive but great quality steaks. No matter your logo style:

You need logo elements that communicate the brand promise.

As in the above examples, these can be icons, graphics, mascots or those vomit-stained doodles from when you came up with your business idea - at midnight after a drinking binge. But keep in mind:

Logos are hard to change, so being specific is limiting as a brand evolves.

For example, if you sell bags and your logo contains a bag, that's fine. But if you move into shoes, the bag won't cover your brand promise anymore. So there's a clear trade-off to make:

Be specific to immediately convey the brand promise, or be vague to remain flexible.

So let's dig up some inspiration.

- ✓ Select some ready-made logos. Browse sites with logo templates 🔧 and enter the keyword that is most relevant to your business, like "cow".
- ✓ There are rich collections online where you can find icons 🔧 that can represent your brand promise, like "steak".
- ✓ Mascots are called "characters" in design land. You can source these illustrations at any major stock photo site 🔧.
- ✓ Get some quality free fonts licensed for commercial work 🔧. Read about fonts before you select something inappropriate.
- ✓ For colors, check out your own mood board and read the chapter on colors.

Paste everything you found in a PowerPoint (.PPT) for future reference and call it "Logo Inspiration". Do not forget to add the links to the locations of your diamonds.

Step 3: Source your logo

By now, you should have all the necessary ingredients for a powerful logo. Or at least a logo which doesn't suck:

1. Some (basic) knowledge about your market.
2. One or more favorite logo types.
3. A brand name.
4. A slogan (or war cry).
5. (PANTONE) Colors.
6. Fonts.
7. Inspiration for graphics, icons or mascots.

Now it's time to make it happen.

Option I: Do it yourself.

Keep sketching until you come up with something worth converting to digital form. But what if you don't have any (digital) drawing skills? Don't panic. Most people couldn't draw a proper stickman at gunpoint.

"Unsatisfactory."

You have to be clever in another way. Let's look at the other ways of sourcing a logo.

Option II: Online logo maker ($10 - $50)

If you are truly down on your luck, and your poverty in ambition is equaled only by your actual poverty, you can try talking to a machine and see what it comes up with. Google one and let it regurgitate your own input for a small amount of money.

Option III: Pay someone ($30 - $100.000)[14]

The old-fashioned way. You brief someone with the above ingredients at a Freelancer site and she'll get to work. If you tap an agency or other creative strategists (like me) for the job it might set you back a fair bit, so measure your budget.

Also, if you are unhappy with the work, you'll have nothing but a worthless scribble and a fat invoice. Designers are humans and humans have uninspired days, so past performance is no guarantee for future returns.

Option IV: Put out a competition ($300 - $700)

You can pay a website to put out a competition. This is a great way to get a lot of designs for little money.

You can dismiss the designs you dislike and get new iterations on the ones you do. Be detailed in your brief, for the ancient adage "sh*t in, sh*it out", holds very true here.

Option V: Buy one ($15 - $350)

The easiest and cheapest way to procure your logo is to buy one from a design database. You will own all the rights, and so does anybody else who buys them.

Your uniqueness will suffer but you're up and running within a minute. Naturally, you can change some colors and shapes around to give it your own flavor, all at little to no cost.

Needless to say, the creative process is open for a combination of these options. You can build a briefing by writing out a competition, and give the best results to a designer, doing it yourself when all else fails.

There were the options to source your logo. For every option goes:

The more invested you are in the process, the more likely you get results.

Step 4: Choose the logo preferred by your audience

Preferably, you end up with multiple logo's to choose from. The designer will always be biased towards his own work – and you are too invested in the process to offer unbiased judgment. So let's test which logo works best.

Use a tool ⊘ to do a preference test.

Some suggested questions:

- Which design do you prefer?
- Which design looks most [insert brand promise like trustworthiness]?
- What do you like / dislike?

The preference of the audience should outweigh personal preferences.

Step 5: Present your logo (Optional)

When presenting your choices, it helps to have a mockup ⊘. These are pictures which contain placeholders for your logo.

It helps people imagine how your logo looks in a piece of context like a product or a business card.

For example, a mockup of a logo can show a picture of a business card with your logo rendered on it.

"It's a mockup of a guy holding a mockup of a guy holding a mockup of our milk bottle."

Step 6: Finalize your logo

Did you settle on a logo? Nice! Now it's time to finalize and save your work.

A. Get a version of your logo with negative colors.

This allows you to put the logo on colored or black backgrounds, increasing its flexibility.

B. Get a horizontal and a vertical version of your logo.

You can now use your logo in every space, be it a website header (horizontal version) and your restaurant menu (vertical version).

C. Get a vector image of your logo in each color type.

All your logos should be delivered as a vector image (.AI or .EPS). These are infinitely scalable and usable for your entire Brand Experience.

Summary and steps for designing a powerful logo

A logo allows your audience to identify your brand. It can be specific to immediately convey the brand promise or be vague to remain flexible. There are 7 different logo types, each used by the world's biggest brands.

- ☑ Step 1: Choose a type of logo.
- ☑ Step 2: Find inspiration for your logo.
- ☑ Step 3: Source your logo.
    - I.   Do it yourself
    - II. Online logo maker ($10 - $50)
    - III. Pay someone ($30 - $100.000)
    - IV. Put out a competition ($300 - $700)
    - V.   Buy one ($15 - $350)
    - VI. Combined approach
- ☑ Step 4: Choose the logo preferred by your audience.
- ☑ Step 5: Present your logo (Optional)
- ☑ Step 6: Finalize your logo.
    - A. Get a version with negative colors.
    - B. Get a horizontal and a vertical version.
    - C. Get a vector image.

Save your work. Put the logos in a folder called "/brandname/identity/logo".

Include both the vector images (.AI / .EPS) as rasterized images with transparent background in high resolution (.PNG).

5.6. How to choose the right fonts

"Good artists borrow, great artists steal."

Pablo Picasso

Were you ever impressed by a monk's manuscript? Annoyed when confronted with an ugly series of characters? Soothed by a social media quote in curvy letters? Then you know the power of fonts.

Your brand uses fonts to communicate its promise.

In this chapter I will:
- ✓ Define the types of fonts.
- ✓ Discuss the different font styles.
- ✓ Stress the necessity of a font hierarchy.
- ✓ Show you where to find fonts for your brand.

You can download a worksheet 🔧 for fonts at www.brandbuilding.com.

The four font flavors

Some typography "experts" say each font deserves their own category. But since we are building a brand and not a dungeon for font lovers, we won't bother with their lingo-heavy fetish.

However, every brand builder should remember 4 terms.

Serif

Serif fonts have 'feet' at the ends of their letters. They evoke tradition, reliability, integrity, and authority. This is why they are used by print media brands and law firms.

Serif fonts express safety and reliability, increasing trust.

The downside is that they can feel dated and old-fashioned. Serif is less suited for small texts on apps or websites since screens can make them look noisy.

Sans-serif

As obvious to you Francophiles, sans-serif fonts do not have any 'feet'. They are the default for cool startups like yours looking to bolster their innovative credentials.

Sans-serif fonts bring a modern, stylish and clean feel.

They are a safe choice for most brands, for they are multi-purpose and neutral. However, the downside is that most Sans-serif can feel bland.

Script

Script fonts look like handwriting and often have connecting letters. Outside of titles, they are used for tooltips, illustrations or descriptions.

Script fonts stand for playfulness and accessibility.

However, they are hard to read and therefore unsuitable for body text. Older people struggle with them for lack of patience and eyesight so use them with restraint.

DISPLAY

Display or decorative fonts are exotic and unusual, designed to be special. They often mix things up, so they do not fall into a clear category.

Display fonts bring a unique flavour and catch the attention.

They can be used for logos and titles, but are wholly unsuited for body text. The downside of their unicity is that they evoke strong opinions and can limit appeal.

As you decorate your ice cream with sprinkles, you can enhance your font flavor with styles.

Most serif and sans-serif fonts come in a 'family' of (1) style and (2) weight options.

Script and display fonts do not, so they are less versatile.

1. **Styles are italics, small capitals, or condensed or extended versions.**

- *"Italics"* are for emphasis, quotes, foreign words, and phonetic sounds.
- *"Small caps"* are uppercase letters matching the height of the lowercase letters. They aren't used often.
- *"Condensed or extended"* versions use less or more space between letters. Not crucial, since most software lets you define this yourself.

2. **Weight means the thickness of each letter like thin, regular or bold.**

- *"Bold/black/heavy"* fonts are easier to read, used for titles or to stress a message.
- *"Regular/medium"* fonts are used for body text.
- *"Thin/hairline"* fonts are for elegant titles and not much else.

You can also change the color intensity of each font.

- *"Light"* fonts are closer to white. They are milder.
- *"Dark"* fonts are closer to black. They are more intense.

Finally, fonts are sized and spaced by "points".

The more points, the bigger the font or space between them. Spacing between sentences is also called *"line height"*.

Now you know the lingo of fonts. Recite it until you can dream it.

"UGH! I dreamed I choose
Comic Sans for my brand..."

Now let's discuss their proper use.

Why you need a font hierarchy

A font hierarchy guides the attention of your audience.

It shows them where to look and what's important. By changing font, size, color and/or style, you make them absorb your information faster:

Without font hierarchy

Berlin walltumbles!
'Beginning of the end'
for communism
Berlin - Forty-five years after it
was divided in defeat and dis-
grace, Germany was reunited
today in a jubilous celebration.
President Weizsacker proclaimed
from the steps of the Reichstag:
"We want to serve peace in the
world of a united Europe."

With font hierarchy

BERLIN WALL TUMBLES!
'Beginning of the end'
for communism
Berlin - Forty-five years after it
was divided in defeat and dis-
grace, Germany was reunited
today in a jubilous celebration.
President Weizsacker proclaimed
from the steps of the Reichstag:
"We want to serve peace in the
world of a united Europe."

Within a hierarchy, every font has a job.
- Headers contain the reason for bothering. They should be immediately visible and very easy to read.
- Subheaders structure your design into sections and group information.
- Body fonts are for the meat of your design, the paragraphs.

Always use the same font in the same style for the same purpose.

Don't use different styles for brochures and website headers. If you mix things up, your brand will have the visual cohesion of a ransom note.

Pro tip: use a spicy decorative font
for a cohesive looking threat.

Step 1: Create a font hierarchy

The next page has an example of a font hierarchy for a fictional restaurant.

You need to create a similar font hierarchy.

For each purpose you must define:
1. A font, including its family name.
2. A size, including different sizes for print, desktops (large screens) and tablets or mobiles (small screens).
3. A color.
4. A line height, including different spacing for print, desktops (large screens) and tablets or mobiles (small screens).
5. A style, defining if you can use dots or italics or other elements per purpose.

PURPOSE	FONT	SIZES	COLOR	LINE HEIGHT	STYLE
ACTION FONT	Londrina Solid	Print: 36 px Desktop: 48 px Tablet / Phone: 32 px	Dim Black	Print: 45 px Desktop: 50 px Tablet / Phone: 40 px	Always without dot
H1 Titles	Francois One	Print: 36 px Desktop: 48 px Tablet / Phone: 32 px	Dim Black	Print: 45 px Desktop: 50 px Tablet / Phone: 40 px	Always without dot
H2 Titles	Francois One	Print: 24 px Desktop: 36 px Tablet / Phone: 26 px	Shadow	Print: 30 px Desktop: 45 px Tablet / Phone: 30 px	Always without dot
H3 Titles	Francois One	Print: 18 px Desktop: 28 px Tablet / Phone: 22 px	Flat Silver	Print: 22 px Desktop: 35 px Tablet / Phone: 25 px	Always without dot
Body text goes like this.	Lato Regular	Print: 12 px Desktop: 16 px Tablet / Phone: 16 px	Mate Grey	Print: 15 px Desktop: 22 px Tablet / Phone: 20 px	Italics where appropriate.
Body highlights go likes this.	Lato Bold	Print: 12 px Desktop: 16 px Tablet / Phone: 16 px	Crimson	Print: 15 px Desktop: 22 px Tablet / Phone: 20 px	No italics in highlight text.
Disclaimers are done in bold like this.	Lato Bold	Print: 10 px Desktop: 14 px Tablet / Phone: 14 px	Dim Black	Print: 12 px Desktop: 17 px Tablet / Phone: 17 px	No italics in disclaimers.

Unsure about size or spacing? Use the best practice numbers in the table.

Feel free to be creative, but you don't have to re-invent the wheel.

Some do's and don'ts for your font hierarchy:
- ✓ Do add color to distinguish yourself.
- ✓ Do light up / add white to your body text to contrast it from the headers.
- ✓ Do light up / add white to colorful headers. Intense fonts can feel tacky.
- ✓ Do light up / add white to your text to make it feel more modern.
- ✓ Do make sure your body font includes regular, bold and italics.
- ✓ Do experiment. You won't get it right on your first run.
- ✗ Do not use thin fonts for medium or small text sizes.
- ✗ Do not use light fonts for small text sizes.
- ✗ Do not use light fonts on a light color or light background.
- ✗ Do not use thin or light fonts everywhere. They'll lose their effect.
- ✗ Do not use decorative or script fonts for body text.

Step 2: Make a selection of fonts for your hierarchy

Finding the right fonts for a brand requires taste, experience, instinct, and experimentation. Start by browsing a font database 🔧.

These sites have thousands of free fonts, are easy to navigate, offer previews with your own text and make downloading easy and quick.

The moment you dive into these libraries, you are bound to be distracted by all the choices. You will love and hate many of them. Just keep the most essential point in mind:

Your fonts must evoke, or at least not contradict, your brand promise.

Your header fonts should be capable of making the right impression. They contain the most important information and will take up most of the real estate in your designs.

Your body font should be non-distracting so your users can easily skim or read your text. It should also perform well in small sizes.

Fonts can be expensive, especially if you go after famous fonts. Some even require multiple licenses.

If you're on a budget or want to keep things simple, stick to free fonts.

Yet as the soccer legend Johan Cruijf said: *"Every upside has its downside."*

While you don't have to pay for testing or using them, they are more common since more brands inevitably use free ones.

Step 3: Ensure legal use

Free fonts can often be used for everything, including commercial purposes. They only prevent you from selling the font itself. However:

Always check and download the licenses of your fonts. Protect yourself.

Also, don't assume that if you pay for a font, you are done thinking. These sometimes require separate licenses, for example for websites and print. Or you have to pay more with more website traffic.

If you want to keep it simple and cheap, stick to free fonts.

And hot dogs.

Step 4: Test your font choices

Perhaps you managed to create multiple font lists, or with some variation in the size, color, spacing, and style. As with colors, these options aren't tested without examples.

Therefore I recommend writing up a (dummy) text that includes the most important elements:

- ✓ Your H1 Title
- ✓ Your H2 Title
- ✓ Your body text

Use a tool 🔵 to let your audience pick their favorite hierarchy.

The questions should be:

- Which text do you like best? (A ranking where respondents place your dummy texts in order of preference.)
- Any suggestions for improvement? (A comment box where they can leave their thoughts.)

Summary and steps for choosing fonts for your brand

Your brand uses fonts to communicate its promise. A font hierarchy - with a font for each purpose - guides the attention of your audience.

- ☑ Step 1: Create a font hierarchy.
- ☑ Step 2: Make a selection of fonts for your hierarchy.
- ☑ Step 3: Ensure legal use.
- ☑ Step 4: Test your font choices.

Save your work. Download and save your fonts (.TTF or .OTF) in a folder called: "/brandname/identity/fonts/".

Download and save your licenses in a folder called: "/brandname/identity/fonts/licenses/".

5.6. How to get powerful images

"A picture is a poem without words."

Horace

Brands rely on powerful images to convey meaning and emotion.

That's why composing and sourcing images are important skills for brand builders. Images are both the taste and the crunch of your brand.

In this chapter, we'll explore how to wield their power and how to source them cheaply.

In this chapter I will:
- ✓ Tell you when to use which type of image.
- ✓ Lay out some general rules for composing images.
- ✓ Show you how to source images.

When to use photos, illustrations and 3D renders

Images come in three formats: photos, illustrations, and 3D renders.
- 3D renders make a 3D model look realistic by adding textures and light.
- Illustrations are drawings, often done digitally.
- Photos are whatever is left of your great-grandmother. My condolences.

"Speak for yourself, sonny boy!"

When you should use photos:
- For accuracy. Your audience will trust a photo to depict a place or product honestly. That's why they are the best choice for selling physical things.
- To provoke visceral reactions. Photos grab the attention quicker than an illustration does. They are best at delivering emotion.
- To look serious. Since photos depict reality the most accurately, they are important for companies that want seriousness in their brand, like investment bankers and lawyers.

When you should use illustrations
- To simplify things (like software). Most software businesses use illustrations to dumb down their interface. They allow you to remove any clutter, presenting your (complex) product as something simple and intuitive.
- For charts, graphs, infographics, or typographic images. They can be used as an overlay for photos and 3D renders as well.
- For fantasy scenes. Photos can destroy much of the magic because they allow little room for the imagination. So whatever leans on illusions must use illustrations.
- To distinguish your brand. Illustrations can be a great way to do something different in a crowded market. When everybody is taking the same photographs, illustrations can bring a whole style and perspective.
- For icons. Icons are simple abstractions. They allow your audience to absorb much information without reading.
- For a vintage look. For much of the last century, advertising was done with illustrations of products and characters. You can mimic their look with your own.

When you should use 3D renders
- For taking an advance on reality. 3D renders can be used to depict a product when there is none yet.
- For products in web stores. You can cheaply and easily render a product in multiple colors, in the perfect composition.

Powerful images convey the brand promise on their own, without the need for long explanations or catchy slogans.

But what is the powerful image? That's a hard question.

As Supreme Court justice Potter Stewart answered when asked to define pornography: *"I know it when I see it."*

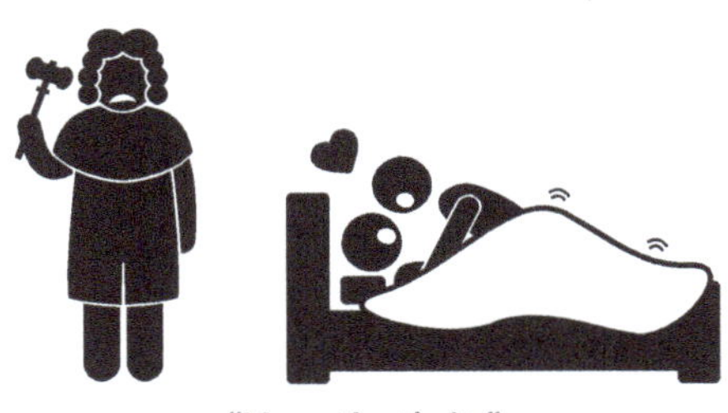

"Yup, that's it."

Likewise, it is hard to define what makes images great. They just stick in our minds and inspire us to commit to a brand. It is hard to define the formula for one, but as the wise justice said: you'll know it when you'll see it.

You need to imagine which composition conveys the brand promise.

Which people are in the image? Where are they? What are they doing? What are they wearing? What emotions are they experiencing? Are they looking into the camera or away from it? What humor, drama or romance can you depict?

You can also study your competitor's photos. Are they showing what you would show? What are they doing wrong? What are they doing right?

Let's list the rules for composing a powerful image:

A. Avoid 'stocky' photos.

We've all seen the polished people with blank eyes and fake smiles. Yuck. Even Disney has the common courtesy to add villains. Cheesy stock does nothing for your audience. Worse, they can create aversion to your brand.

"Surely this can be used
to sell 1,000 different products."

B. Never compromise on quality.

Avoid low-quality images. They will do more harm than good. So make sure your object is well-lit, in focus and has good resolution. (At least 72 dpi for online, preferably 300 dpi for print).

The pose for quality images.
Or so I assume.

C. Don't bore or freak out your audience.

People are bored by large crowds (there's no one to focus on) and historical subjects (no clear relevance to their life). Then, close-ups of faces are experienced as slightly grotesque. (Especially yours.)

Also, try to stay away from violence.

And yes, dodgeball is a form of voilence.

D. Use depth-of-field.

Depth-of-field is your magic bullet. By making sure your object is in focus and the background isn't, you quickly evoke a professional feeling. Many consumer-grade camera's offers this function, so use it whenever possible.

Foreground: sharp. Background: blurry.

E. Use emotion.

People react strongly to people. This is just how the brain fires. So the emotion evoked by your image is immediately felt by your audience. This helps to grab their attention.

Make sure it's the emotion your brand needs to convey. If you're selling designer handbags, arouse a haughty sense of style. If you're running a charity, you'll want to inspire a crippling sense of sadness.

Sad already, are you?
Then go Google a charity!

F. Picture your audience.

If your audience consists of baby-boomers, don't show millennials. Make sure you depict people, situations, and emotions your customers can relate to, and make it feel real.

If you are mixing audiences, be sure the group composition doesn't raise any questions.

Something feels off here...

G. Create dead space for text.

Text in an image is always read by your audience. Text beside, above, underneath or behind an image isn't.

Therefore, try to achieve some 'dead space' in the composition of your image. This is an area where nothing is happening so I can insert text without a noisy background distracting from it.

You can move elements and extend photos by cloning entire parts of it. (Using Photoshop) This is the easiest way to make room for your message.

Stretching the sky to create room for text.

H. Add action.

If there is some visceral motion going on in the picture, people know there is a story being told. Movement means energy and energy means attention.

Action makes everything interesting.
Even baseball.

You have composed your images in your mind or on paper. You now know what you want. Let's go get it!

Sourcing photos

Option I. Browse the stock databases ($0 - $50 per photo)

The internet is littered with free and paid images that you can use for your brand. These stock photos are cheap and instantly ready for use.

However, they are very generic because they have to be widely applicable and non-offensive. You will never find the exact composition you have in mind as a stock photo. But perhaps something close to it.

Search the (free) stock photo sites 🔗. Use keywords from your composition to see how close you can get, like "female pool book" or "friends drinking phone".

Search and save many of them. That way you have something to choose.

After settling on one, use Photoshop to add elements from your brand in the picture. This can be a logo on a window or your mascot in a background photo. If people recognize your Brand Identity in the photo, they are more easily persuaded it's your own creation.

Option II: download a mockup ($0 - $50 per photo)

If your composition involves the use of a digital product or service, like an app or a webshop, you can download screen mockups 🔗. These show a screen in the desired environment, easily replaced with your interface.

Search for "iPad mockup grass" or "desktop mockup senior" to get close to your composition. The screens are smart objects in Photoshop, replaced within a minute.

Option III: shoot them yourself ($100 - $10,000 per photoshoot)

If you want the ideal composition, you'll have to start from scratch. This means recruiting the people, finding the props and scouting the location yourself.

You'll also need a real camera and – if you are not shooting in bright daylight – a set of lights. Hiring a photographer who provides these can be a safe choice. Make sure (1) she has the experience (does she have similar compositions in his portfolio?) and (2) is willing to transfer all the photos, rights-free, after the shoot.

However, photographers often have only rudimentary Photoshop skills. They can enhance brightness and colors, but cannot add props, 3D renders or other composition elements.

That's why post-production is best done by yourself or another party. You are then free to be very selective and demanding.

Then, since you are spending some serious time and money to set the stage right, why don't you shoot some video? You can make a proper commercial or recycle the material into GIFs.

Option IV: ask an agency to produce them ($2,500 and up)

The biggest brands with the biggest budgets ask the best agencies to produce their images. The entire production, shoot, and editing are outsourced to a (hopefully) competent party who will produce the exact series of images you need for your brand.

Yet, just as with photographers, be sure to brief them thoroughly. Verify if they can produce the quality and scope you have in mind by checking their portfolio. And join them on the shoot to make sure they stick to your vision.

Also, acquire all the material for the shoot for your digital archive. You never know when you need more content.

As for photos, start with the composition. What elements will convey your brand promise?

Option I: Draw them yourself.

Yeah, right. This requires a lot of time and talent. It's unlikely you have both.

Option II: Download multiple illustrations and combine them ($0 - $200)

Illustrations are free ⦿ or available for purchase through sites for stock photos ⦿ and graphic assets ⦿. But unlike photos, images can be easily taken apart, their elements combined into your composition.

This you can source each element of your composition separately, and combine them to create perfection. You need to be skilled in Adobe Illustrator or other vector-based software to do this.

Let's do this!

Then, style each element according to your Brand Identity. Harmonize line size and colors. Add or strip gradients and shadows. Make sure each element feels a part of your brand.

Option III: Pay someone ($0 - $1,000)

There are some highly skilled illustrators on the internet. Since their line of work is saturated with hopefuls, they come cheap.

Make sure their portfolio contains the quality and style you are looking for. Or even better, ask the illustrator of your favorite stock illustrations to draw yours. They aren't expensive.

Then deliver a comprehensive briefing. The more creative freedom you allow, the more likely the result will stray from your vision.

The 'children's friend'
you had in mind.

The 'children's friend'
that is delivered.

Sourcing 3D renders

For the 3D rendering of your product, you need a 3D model of it. For now, I'll assume you have one.

As before, proceed to imagine the perfect composition for your 3D renders to express your brand promise.

I recommend including your render in a photo or 3D environment for added realism. This creates the illusion of a product available and in use.

You can source environments from 3D asset sites ⊘ or stockphoto sites ⊘.

Needless to say, the product has to look realistic within your composition. So pay extra attention by adding shadows, reflections, and other effects so your 3D render 'interacts' with the environment.

Remove the fruit bowl and add a your toaster.
Then blur the image above the toaster to simulate heat.

Option I: Render it yourself.

If you can both do 3D renders and Photoshop, try doing it yourself.

Option II: Get a freelancer. ($200 - $1,000)

Adding your product to a 3D environment or photo requires some expertise, which freelancers ⊘ offer online.

For including your product in a 3D environment, find a freelancer who does architectural visualizations.

For including your product in a photo, you need a freelancer with both 3D rendering skills and advanced Photoshop skills.

Don't settle for work that doesn't fool your family.

Step 3: Buy and save your licenses

Can you use (stock) images without buying them? Yes. But it can get you in big trouble.

Stock image sellers like Getty Images use reverse images search.

They continuously scan the internet for clandestine use of their images. When they suspect wrongdoing, their legal team will viciously strongarm you until you fork over a heft bribe.

Don't ask me how I know.

For other websites with widely used photos, this practice is less common.

I've never heard of a case where copying illustrations was punished.

However:

Make sure you buy and save a license of every image you use.

It's called image lawyer immunity.

Step 4: Enhance your images in post-production

There's a girl in the movie Gia complaining about unrealistic beauty standards: *"Magazines don't come with a label saying, 'Caution: This is a lie. Nobody looks like this.'" Then she turns to Angelina Jolie, saying: "Not even you."*

That statement testifies to Photoshop's ability to optimize images and inspire depression. Of course, like a sharp blade, it can be used for good or for evil. And lucky for the world, we're the good guys.

I wish my life was like that...

To master the basics of Photoshop is to wield the same power. You can:

- Combine the best parts of multiple attempts at a photo. (Select and cut)
- Add elements from other photos. (Select and cut)
- Remove blemishes from the actors and the environment. (Clone stamp)
- Suck that gut in and broaden those shoulders. (Warp)
- Extend the photo to generate dead space for text. (Clone stamp)
- Increase brightness, vibrancy, and contrast. (Add layer)
- Add photo effects to convert elements into sketch, smoke or sparkles. (Search for "Photoshop Actions")

Go easy on the filters. They are inappropriate unless you're posting to a millennial wine bar's Instagram.

"And I was like: what-evs Susan!"

Step 5: Optimize your images for online use

Search engines prefer high-resolution images. The JPEG file format provides the best quality and the smallest file size. PNGs can be a good alternative, but try using PNG-8 over PNG-24.

You also want to compress your images to increase load speed. There are tools ⊘ to help you out.

When uploading them, you can add a concise caption. These, like URLs, can be crawled by search engines and are read 3x more often than the body copy itself.

Summary and steps for choosing images for your brand

Brands rely on powerful images to convey meaning and emotion. They come in three formats: photos, illustrations, and 3D renders. Powerful compositions convey the brand promise on their own, without the need for long explanations or catchy slogans.

- ☑ Step 1: Compose powerful images
- ☑ Step 2: Source your compositions
  Sourcing photos:
  I. Browse the stock databases ($0 - $50 per photo)
  II. Download a mockup ($0 - $50 per photo)
  III. Shoot them yourself ($100 - $10,000 per photoshoot)
  IV. Ask an agency to produce them ($2,500 and up)
  Sourcing illustrations:
  I. Draw them yourself.
  II. Download multiple illustrations and combine them ($0 - $200)
  III. Pay someone ($0 - $1,000)
  Sourcing 3D renders:
  I. Render it yourself.
  II. Get a freelancer. ($200 - $1,000)
- ☑ Step 3: Buy and save a license for every image you use.
- ☑ Step 4: Enhance your images in post-production
- ☑ Step 5: Optimize your images for online use

Save your work materials like stock photos and Photoshop work files (.PSD & .JPEG) in a folder called: "/brandname/images/source"

Download and save your licenses in a folder called: "/brandname/images/source/licenses"

Save your images to be used in a folder called: "/brandname/images/"

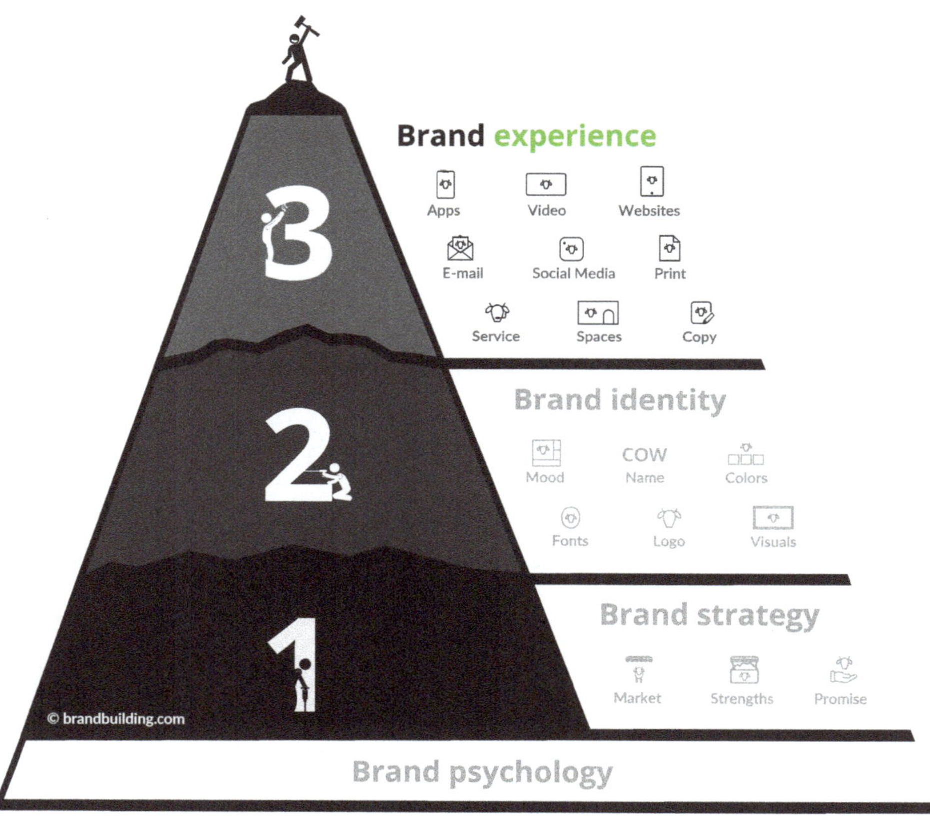
Brand experience
3
Apps
Video
Websites
E-mail
Social Media
Print
Service
Spaces
Copy
Brand identity
2
Mood
COW
Name
Colors
Fonts
Logo
Visuals
Brand strategy
1
Market
Strengths
Promise
© brandbuilding.com
Brand psychology

6. Brand experience (Stage 3)

6.1. Introduction

"Your brand is a story unfolding across all customer touchpoints."

Jonah Sachs

Imagine encountering a perfectly polished cow.

Her strong back arches towards the sky. The full calves provide a strong grip, and two horns shine brightly in the mid-morning sun, proudly piercing the dust of the busy market.

Its majesty speaks to your highest aspirations, and the promise of a brighter tomorrow has you open up your wallet.

Ahem. Let's just say that a great Brand Experience has an emotional impact. You're transported into the domain of irrationality, where feelings override reason. The rational part of your brain tags along for the ride as you commit to the project in front of you.

Someone transported by
a magical brand experience.

In the previous parts, we decided on a brand promise and composed the basic ingredients of Brand Identity.

In this stage we build a Brand Experience to get your audience to commit.

However, some of the chapters might be more relevant than others. To identify which matter most to your brand, you can map a *customer journey*.

A customer journey is a list of all the touchpoints with your audience.

You'll need to identify where they come from and how they move towards commitment.

Here's a simplified example of your favorite soda:

Together, these touchpoints form your Brand Experience.

A great Brand Experience convinces the audience to commit at each and every touchpoint.

This stage is about getting each of them right. So let's get to it!

6.2. How to make a website

"Make it simple, but significant."

Don Draper

Every brand has a website getting the audience to buy, sign up, donate, volunteer or vote. These 'conversions' are the goal.

Your website is the online backbone of your brand.

First, it gives an overview of your brand and its promise. Then, it gently guides your audience to a commitment, with a signup form or a web store. Finally, it's a tool to analyze your user needs and preferences. That's why:

We'll start building your Brand Experience by making a website.

In this chapter I will:
- ✓ Outline some rules for websites.
- ✓ Warn you about agencies building your website.
- ✓ Show you the steps for designing and building a website.

The steps in this chapter will produce an affordable, user-friendly website that converts your audience. Ignore these steps and you'll probably end up with an expensive mess that does nothing but damage to your brand.

Good website

User stay and commit.

Bad website

Users leave and fume.

Rules for websites

Website functionality and design changes at a breakneck pace.

Yet people are still people. Their patience and capacity to process information are limited. Their fingers remain the same size. They still decide if they want to stay on your site within a few seconds. That's why:

The principles of making websites remain the same.

Let's explore a few of them, and draw some conclusions as we go.

I'll rewrite this chapter when we'll get neural interfacing.

Users leave quick or stay long

The internet is of highly variable quality. Everyone knows this. That's why:

Users spend their initial moments on your website in ruthless judgment.

Their only question: is this site useful or should I abort my visit?

Start with the wrong note and get cancelled.

The time spend on your website follows a Weibull distribution . The likelihood of leaving decreases with each second spent on your site. Users grow optimistic over time, much like the merciless judges on your favorite talent show.

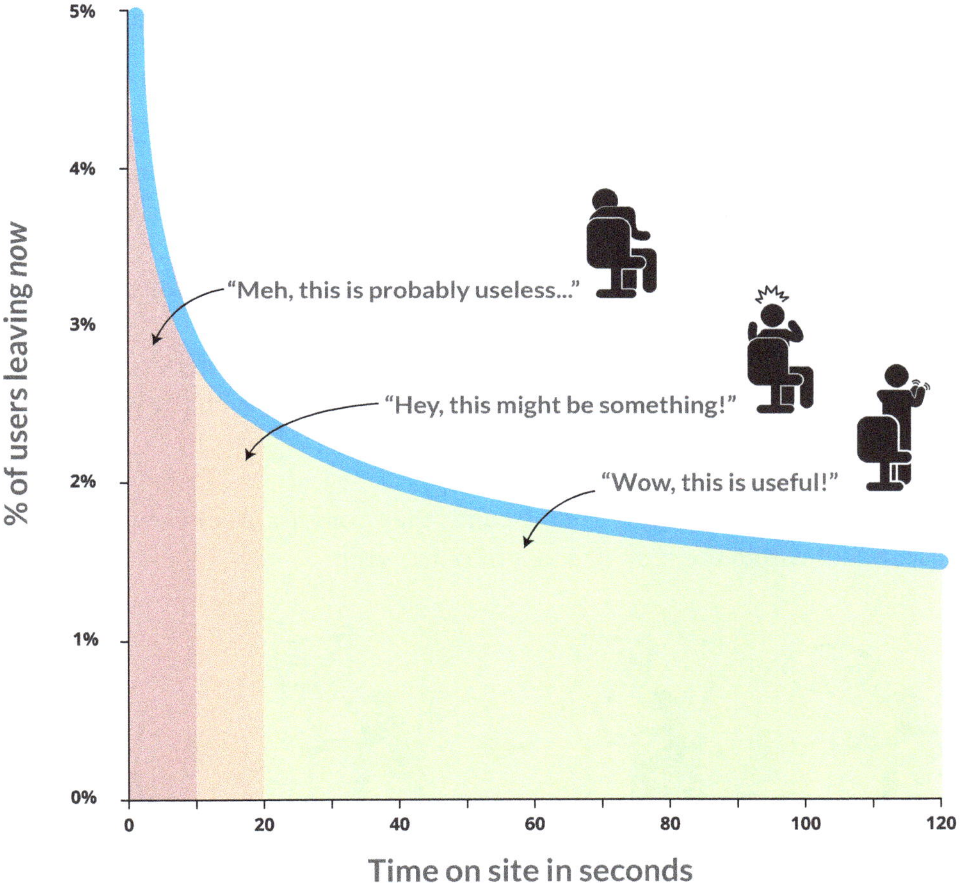

The first 10 to 20 seconds on your website are critical.

However, if you manage to survive them, users can be willing to spend 2 minutes or more, an eternity on the internet.

Your user is always on a quest for relevancy. If the site is not relevant to her needs, she will bail.

To judge relevancy, users compare the words in mind with those on screen.

There should be a perfect match. If a user searches for 'dog food', your text should include the words 'dog food'. These keywords contain a wealth of knowledge and associations, without you having to explain anything.

Use keywords in your header. Not synonyms, play-on-words or poetry.

Want 'dog food'? Then 'Pet meals' or 'kibble time' are mismatches. Now users must spend mental energy linking their keywords with the words on your site.

The same goes ads and the landing pages they point to. Avoid any disconnect within the first 20 seconds of the visit.

"I need some dog food"

"Let's search for dog food..."

"This ad says dog food. That's exactly what I need!"

"This site says dog food. I'm in the right place."

There are tools 🔧 to find out what keywords your audience uses.
Use them to decide on what words to employ for your headers and copy.
Also, Search engines will reward content that matches better.

"What the &*@# is kibble time?" What a useless waste of my time!"

Given that your users are just passing by, and even the most generous of them will stay only a few minutes:

Make sure users grab the basics of your brand as they scan your site.

- ✓ Create visual hierarchies by structuring text with (sub)headlines
- ✓ Break your pages up in modules.
- ✓ Make your design as clean as possible by eliminating distractions.

Never underestimate the visitor's need for clarity and brevity. Your visitor prefers to think about things that are easy to think about.

That's why they stay when your website is easy to navigate and understand and leave when it's not. Also:

Cut the waffle. No-one wants to hear you pontificate.

Users visit for their own benefit only.

- ✓ Keep it short & sweet. Every second of attention is precious. Strip *every* superfluous word, sentence, or paragraph.
- ✓ Be generous with headlines and sub-headlines to structure your text.
- ✓ Use bullets instead of long sentences, where possible.

Stuffy paragraphs merely serve as walls of words. They repel your user and give the impression that you need to read everything before committing. Scrap them.

"Those are some intimidating paragraphs. I'm out."

Conventions exist for every type of site: eCommerce, news sites, restaurants, and social media. Others in each category have run countless experiments to figure out the best ways to present information, structure sites and get conversions.

Conventions are your friend if you respect them.

Users have grown to expect websites in each category to feel and work a certain way. Every time you ignore a convention, they will need to learn something new.

User time and patience are best spent on your brand promise.

Don't waste their cognitive ability by defying convention. If you do, be very sure there is (a) little learning curve and (b) the extra value is worth the friction. Since these are generous assumptions:

You are better off borrowing the best practices from your competitors.

Be strict with creative agencies. They don't get peer recognition, industry awards or an exotic portfolio by meekly following 'convention'. Nor can they bill a lot of hours. These are strong incentives to ignore what's been tried and tested.

Creative gets an award
for 're-imagining the web'.

User can't find
the goshdarn basics.

Mobile first

Finally, this is a mobile-first world. Even though you'll design on a laptop or desktop, your visitors are most likely to come by phone.

Prioritize how your website looks and feels on smaller screens.

- ✓ *Make it fast.* Loading speed matters for users and search engine rankings. Compress your images and use caching.
- ✓ *Make it readable.* Smaller screens need large buttons and large text.
- ✓ *Make it responsive.* Have your layouts adjust automatically to any screen size, whether it's a desktop, laptop, tablet, or mobile phone. Most templates and website builders automatically do this.

So design your website with the small screens in mind. Keep testing and optimizing, and not only on the device you're developing on.

Make it work for every screen size.

On having agencies help make a site

We now design your website before we build it, based on the above principles. I'll show them some steps, each of which you can do yourself.

If you're hiring an agency, beware of the ancient trick: quote a small amount based on your initial briefing and explain the need for more hours after the first invoice.

Without a complete briefing, agencies can try to lock you in with low quotes. The solution is to give them a full briefing with a sitemap, wireframes and detailed functionality (step 1 to 3), and ask for a fixed project price.

Step 1: Write down a main measurable purpose (MMP)

You should state a purpose for your website.

Don't worry, this is not some feel-good exercise to get you pumped for the hard work ahead. Defining a purpose is vital, because:

Your site won't do what you want if you don't define what you want.

Who will hit the target?

Sadly, 'something awesome' is not a purpose.

And neither is 'informing and convincing people'.

Your purpose should be singular and measurable.

That's why it's the main measurable purpose (MMP). It provides both guidance and a metric by which to judge your efforts. Do not start building a site without it.

So what will be the MMP of your website?
- For a webshop, this might be turnover.
- For a subscription SaaS business, this might be signups.
- For charitable and political sites, this might be donation volume.

Or it could be brochure downloads, email signups, or incoming calls. You'll notice a pattern:

Your website MMP is all about getting users to commit.

For BrandBuilding.com, the MMP is outbound traffic to booksellers. For Toby, my subscription dog food business, it's 2-week trials.

You also might have secondary objectives, like recruiting talent or raising brand awareness. These are valid, but not as important.

Your entire site should be built towards realizing your MMP.

This is why big companies have a separate recruiting site or different sites for businesses and consumers. It allows them to efficiently move different target groups towards different MMP's.

Step 2: List and structure your pages

Next, you must come up with a page structure that serves your MMP. The fancy word for this is a sitemap. It provides an overview of your site's content and ensures your pages can be intuitively navigated.

A. List all the pages you'll need.

You'll have a 'home page', and perhaps an 'our story', 'referrals', 'shopping cart', or others. Each should contain information that helps your visitor contribute to your MMP.

B. Structure your pages in a tree.

The sitemap can be a template for your navigation structure later.

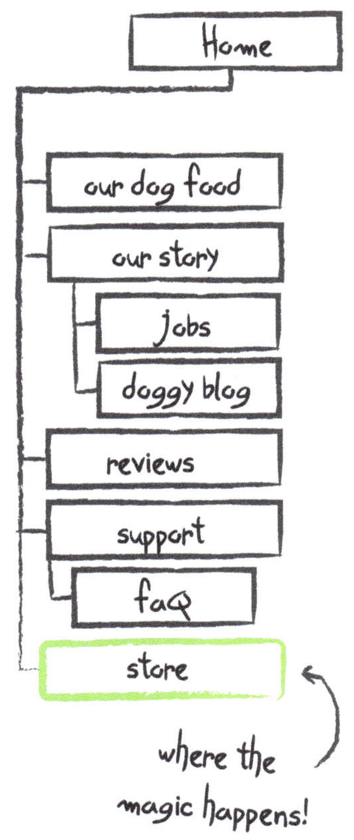

Step 3: Sketch a wireframe for each page

Designing your website is time-consuming. So is building one. That's why you sketch every page first.

These sketches are called 'wireframes'. They allow you to change the layout when it's still cheap and easy to do so.

You should wireframe each page in your sitemap before designing it.

Wireframes give pages a visual structure. They do not include content. Images can be represented with rectangles, whilst text can be visualized with simple lines. You aren't using colors, logos or other artwork.

The shapes only represent these elements on each page.

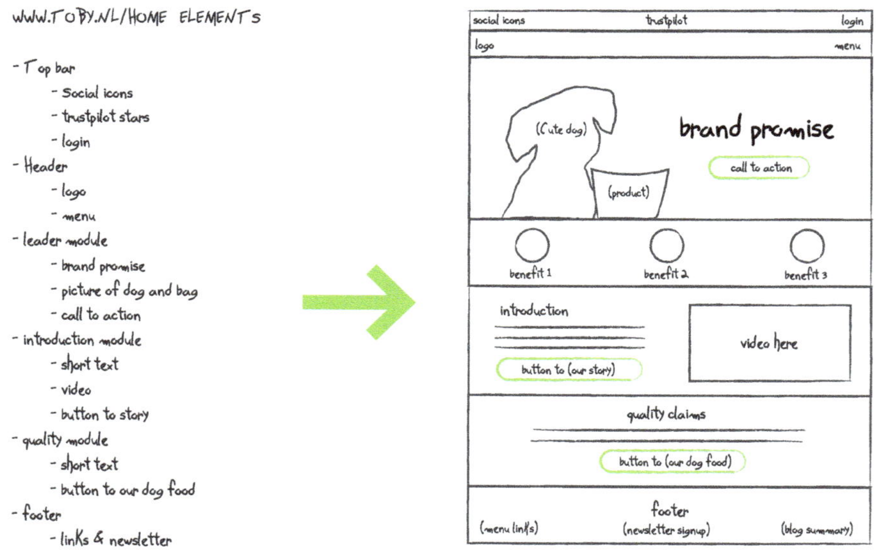

Toby wireframe (simplified)

Don't include design elements. They distract from the purpose, which is deciding where things go, not how things look like. You'll be coloring in the wireframe soon enough.

Wireframes must be in grayscale so only the layout is in focus.

Start again by listing all your elements to include on each page. Next, arrange them. You can use pen and paper, PowerPoint or a tool 🔧.

Naturally, content pages – like news items or case studies – only have to be wireframed once.

Step 4. Design (or prototype) your wireframes

You bring your wireframe to life by adding your design elements. If you've followed these steps, and you have a Brand Identity ready, this step will be easy.

You can design the site in Photoshop based on the wireframes.

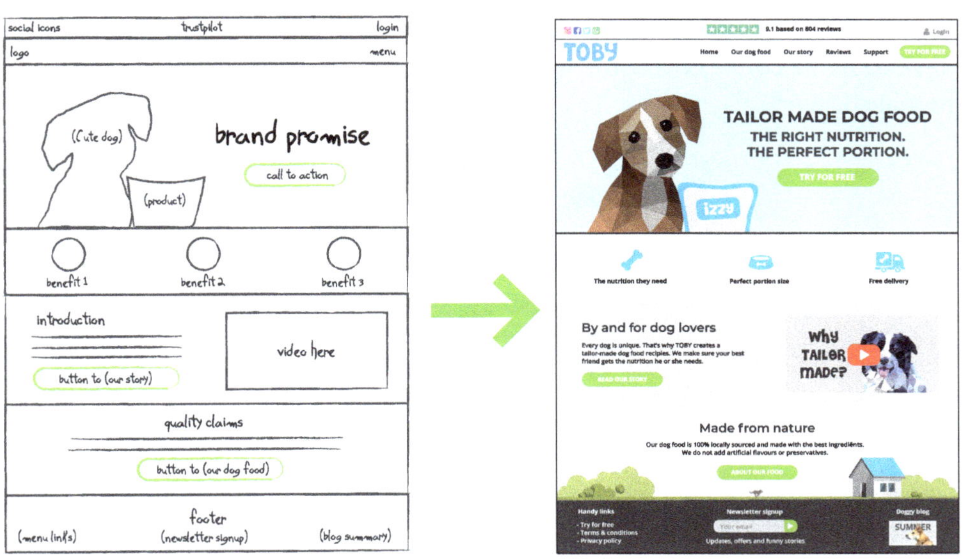

Toby wireframe (simplified)

You can also go one step further and prototype your website. This means using a prototyping tool 🔧 instead of Photoshop. Only do this if you are going for high-end websites because prototyping itself is labor-intensive.

Step 5: Source your website.

There are several options for each ambition level and budget.

Option 1 – Code it yourself

You code from scratch. It's the only way to get an exotic design or special functionality.

If you have coding skills, I don't need to tell you that there are multiple frameworks to choose from, each with libraries to make your life easier.

Code yourself if:
- Your functionality or design demands it AND
- Skills (or funds) are available.

Coders are in demand and thus expensive. If you can't afford them, you'll have to make concessions in your design and functionality. Or sell a kidney to make it work.

"He's going for a
crypto-trading site in Rust."

Option 2 – Use a Content Management System

The design or functionality of 95% of websites does not require coding skills. Both are available as templates or plugins respectively.

Better said, everything you want already exists.

This doesn't mean you aren't creative. You just don't have to re-invent the wheel. Here, I walk with the herd and recommend a Content Management System (CMS) called Wordpress.

A CMS is the Swiss army knife for creating and publishing web pages.

And Wordpress is the most popular version on the internet. More than half (!) of all websites run on Wordpress.

The CMS Wordpress has an ecosystem of free and paid building blocks.

These building blocks make building your website as easy as playing with Lego's. Heck, even my 84-year old grandmother runs a Wordpress-powered site for her paintings.

"Now let me update my conversion analytics plugin before nappy time."

Most designs can be built with a Wordpress drag and drop page builder.

Now take your design wishes: whatever you have in mind, there is a 95% chance it can be built with a drag and drop page builder. I use the Avada template with its Fusion Builder.

Most functionality is available as plugins to Wordpress.

Whatever functionality you have in mind, there is a 95% chance it's available as a (paid) plugin:

✓ eCommerce platforms with subscription options exist.
✓ Real estate websites with listing filters exist.
✓ International trading platforms exist.

Use a CMS if:
- Your functionality is available in Wordpress plugins AND.
- You can learn Wordpress or have some money to pay for these skills.

Option 3 – Use an online website builder

Only need an online presence with no special design or functionality? Use a website builder like www.wix.com or www.squarespace.com.

Pick a website builder's template and jam in your content.

Just strip away what you don't need. Obviously, the templates of website builders won't accommodate anything beyond the basics.

Use a website builder if:
- You have no resources, cognitive or otherwise AND.
- You don't care about how people perceive you AND.
- You only have to show some pictures of your xylophone performance.

Website builders truly are for *everyone.*
(With no offense to my brother Bart)

Kidding aside, website builders are a valid option if both your requirements and your resources are very limited.

Picking a method

No matter the chosen method, there are guides available online to get you started. Go with what your resources and demands dictate, but with no more. There's no need to waste money or time.

Also, if a large chunk of functionality is available within the CMS, you can always opt to have some custom code supplement the available plugins.

	Custom code	CMS	Website builder
Design & functionality options	●●●●	●●●	●
Required skills	●●●●	●●	●
Required time	●●●●	●●	●

Summary and steps for making a website for your brand

Websites must convert your visitor. They are only effective if they are designed for conversions from the beginning.

The principles of websites should be followed at all times. If they are ignored, your user ends up leaving frustrated.

Designing a website is straightforward and easy, and can be done by anyone. Conventions should be respected. Best practices can be borrowed from competitors.

Building a website can require skills, depending on the chosen method. The choice of method should depend on the available resources and the required functionality.

- ☑ Step 1. Write down a main measurable purpose (MMP) for your website.
- ☑ Step 2. List and structure your pages.
    - A. Make a sitemap by listing all the pages you have in mind.
    - B. Structure your pages in a tree.
- ☑ Step 3: Sketch wireframes for each page.
- ☑ Step 4. Design (or prototype) your wireframes.
    - I. Code it yourself (High skill or high budget)
    - II. Use a CMS (Medium skill or medium budget)
    - III. Use an online website builder (No skills or no budget)

6.3. How to write effective copy

"Write the best story that you can and write it as straight as you can."

Ernest Hemmingway

Your brand needs well-chosen words (copywriting) to explain its promise and why you (or your team) is capable to deliver on it.

Effective copy (1) delivers your message *and* (2) strokes the imagination.

If you neglect the first, you aren't converting anybody. No-one reads fat paragraphs vomit-stained with jargon. You need to write in a simple and direct way as if you were having a conversation.

If you fail at the second, nobody reads your stuff. No-one wants to chew through your arid content. Your audience needs the positive emotion that follows warm, funny, honest, fresh or visionary words.

It's hard to brew up words that both sell and inspire.

That's why good copywriters earn great money. But anyone who can string together a sentence can learn to be effective. Hence this chapter. I'll explore:

The basic rules for copywriting.
- ✓ How to obtain copy that sells and inspires.
- ✓ How to test crucial lines of copy.
- ✓ How to design your copy.

Follow the steps and you'll arrive at copy that – in the words of writer Ann Handley – *"explains in human terms how [your brand] adds value to people's lives, eases troubles, shoulders burdens, and meets needs."*

Rules for copywriting

Everybody can write. However, you need some basic rules to avoid boring your audience to death.

A copywriter is a salesman behind a keyboard.

Writing about your brand is about selling it. Nothing else.

Don't be clever or literary. Your job is not to garner poetry accolades or impress your sweetheart. That's a totally different sport. Selling is what matters here.

But if you sell too hard, defenses go up.

People distrust overt sales talk. And for good reason. Everyone has been burned by inaccurate or dishonest copy that overpromised the value of a brand.

The more discreet the sell, the more effective the copy.

So don't put on the hard sell. Have a friendly conversation with your audience. Never boast, pose or brag, because your audience will think you're sleazy.

Also, feel free to use emotional language.

Words like grow, love, heart, needs, driven, goals, choose, join, believe, conversation, personal, smarter, forge, experience are useful in presenting your pitch in a more humane way.

Be real, friendly, authentic, honest and personal.

Instead of writing "Our product increases customer loyalty", write "Built to help you grow customer love."[15]

Instead of writing "This product is really easy to use", write: "We believe power comes from simplicity."[16]

Instead of writing "We have more useful tools besides chat", write: "Come for our chat. Stay for our everything else."[17]

The headline is critical

Your audience has aggressive filters for what deserves their attention. When scanning search results, newspapers or an inbox, the following rule applies:

Five times as many people read the headline as they read what's beneath.

So your headline is the first, and probably only, impression you make on a prospective reader. This makes sense. The headline summarizes why the reader should bother. So if you botch it, nobody will.

This makes writing headlines a critical skill for brand builders.

Whether it's the header on your website or header of an email – it deserves the most attention. Some copywriting legends recommend spending half your time on the piece's headline.

Every line of copy has but one purpose - to get the next sentence read.

This goes for the header and the body copy. Get it read. And then the one after that. And so on, all the way to your call to action. The reason why all many headlines start with "How to", "How", "Why", "Which", "Who else", "This", "Because", "If" or "Advice". It works. Why?

Great copy immediately focusses on the reader's benefit.

I know. Your brand is no clickbait. You don't want your headlines to follow corny formulas. (No judgment if they do. I *was* amazed by how the cast of that 90's show looks now!)

Albert Einstein once said that *"everything should be made as simple as possible, but not simpler."* He grows more right as our attention span withers.

Always write simply and directly.

Intellectual audiences are no exception. Even brainy readers are often so mentally congested that their comprehension drops to the level of a 12-year old.

Make sure your audience 'gets' your brand promise immediately.

The most successful headlines use less than 8 words. If you need more, think harder and come up with shorter versions.

If you can replace a multi-syllable word with a mono-syllable one, do so. Yes, your PhD friends will think you a simpleton, but you're getting your point across just fine.

"Haha! He writes stuff that
commoners understand!"

You can also bend the rules of grammar if it helps to get the message across. Use one-sentence paragraphs, sentence fragments, punctuation, and other magic if it makes your copy easier to digest.

No-one will complain that your copy is too easy. Ever.

You can't just leave it at the headline. When writing the body text underneath it you should:

✓ Keep focussing on the reader's benefit. Never allow them to wonder why they are reading your copy.

✓ Each part of the body copy should support the brand promise by presenting a clear idea or benefit. Don't digress with random stories.

✓ Cut out the fat.

✓ Offer large amounts of credibility whenever you can. Use media references, experts, customer testimonials, case studies and statistics to bolster your claims.

✓ In your conclusion, restate the original reason for your prospect to read your stuff. Summarize your story, showing them that you fulfilled the promise made in the header.

✓ Finally, conclude with an offer or a call to action. Give them guarantees if you can. Pressing that button or filling that form is no small thing.

How to source your copy

There are two ways to get your copy. You can do it yourself, or pay a copywriter.

Doing it yourself has the obvious benefit of being free. But it also saves you from extensively briefing a copywriter – which is necessary if she is to produce anything of value.

Even if you've never written copy before, quality relies more on authenticity and a love for your brand than experience.

What you lack in literary sophistication you can compensate with honesty and labor.

There is no need to know all the words. Besides, there's a thesaurus for that. And if you follow these steps, you are bound to end up with something highly palatable to your audience.

Step 1: List the keywords used by your audience

Keywords are the exact words that your audience uses when searching.

There are free keyword tools ⊘ that list your keywords and their volume for every search engine.

This is invaluable because you can use these words in your headlines. If the customer sees their own words reflected back to them, you catch their attention.
By using the language of your audience, you prove that your brand is relevant to them.

Using keywords online also boosts your brand in search engine rankings. These machines care that the content displayed is relevant, so keyword use weighs heavily in their decision to bump you up in the results.

Of course, never use keywords for the sake of keywords.

Don't jam them into your copy. Sometimes they just don't jive. But keep a list of them handy when composing. If you can include them, all the better.

Step 2: Get inspired

There's no need to re-invent the wheel. Take a look at the most admired brands in your space, and see how they approach their headlines and body copy. Multinationals spend thousands of hours composing and testing their copy.

A. Get inspired by the style and rhythm of other brands.

You can also search for swipe files, which are collections of headlines that worked. The history of advertising copy yielded thousands of do's and don't's, free for you to access.

B. Google "great headline collection" and school yourself.

It's never illegal to get inspired. Stealing is though. So don't just copy other people's work.

"Let's get inspired by this warehouse."

And whatever lessons you take away from the greats, know that there's a sequence of words out there for you that captures your message *just* right.

Step 4: Test crucial copywriting

The major headlines on your website and flagship brochure should be field-tested. You'll want to know what works and what doesn't.

All crucial headlines should be tested.

Testing is cheaper and easier than ever before. Don't skip it, believing that your prose should be exempt from commoner feedback. Also, don't be lazy. Sub-optimal copy can seriously hurt your brand. Make sure it's perfect and on point.

An easy way to test is Google Ads. You deploy multiple ads, each displaying a different version of your headline. The algorithm will rotate them. The one with the highest click-through-rate wins.

You can also run *five second tests* 🔵. Upload screenshots of your copy and see if people 'get' your brand promise within five seconds. The copy that gets the instant understanding wins.

Step 5: Design your copywriting

People judge a book by its cover because they have no time to read every book. And that's fair.

- ✓ Remember the introduction about cows and sh*tstains? Same goes for your copy. Hose it down and make it presentable:
- ✓ Design your text for scanning. Use short paragraphs and many headlines.
- ✓ Use an (online) spellchecker and let someone proofread your work.
- ✓ Use a font that's easy on the eyes and big enough to read. See the chapter on fonts.
- ✓ Use short and/or indented paragraphs.
- ✓ Add relevant images and graphics.
- ✓ Mix it up using bold, italicized, underlined or highlighted words.
- ✓ Add quotes from famous people and or customers.
- ✓ Use visual cues like dividers and arrows, or playful elements like a handwritten signature.
- ✓ Use bullets or numbers to make clear lists. Every sentence with multiple commas is a candidate. (See? Walking the talk.)

Text that looks like a madman's scribble on a truck stop toilet door will be ignored. And so it should.

"OK, now that's just inappropriate…"

So don't drop the design ball. The package is as important as the content.

Summary and steps toward great copy

Effective copy (1) concisely delivers your message and (2) strokes the imagination. Your words should both sell and inspire.

You can write perfectly good copy by observing the rules. Make sure to use a conversational style and to focus on the headline.

- ☑ Step 1: List the keywords used by your audience.
- ☑ Step 2: Get inspired:
    I. Observe the style and rhythm of other brands.
    II. Google "great headline collection" and school yourself.
- ☑ Step 3: Write and weigh every word.
- ☑ Step 4: Test crucial copywriting.
- ☑ Step 5: Design every piece of copy.

Save your work in a folder called "/brandname/copy/".

6.4. How to service your customers

"They may forget what you said, but they'll never forget how you made them feel."
Anonymous

Stories abound of companies destroying the competition by investing in delighting customers. No wonder.

Happy customers buy more and more often, refer their friends and leave good reviews.

Now delighting customers requires doing special things. Otherwise, it wouldn't be delightful. It'd be dead normal.

Do the things big companies can't. Write those notes, make those calls.

Have the customer focus other companies consider excessive. For if you delight your customer, they'll want to delight you too.

By focussing on customer delight, the company morale also improves. It's just fun to make people happy, and:

Happy multiplies, often beyond your wildest expectations.

Unhappy multiplies also. Customers will trash your brand on the internet and elsewhere. You'll clip your own wings if you disappoint instead of delight.

In this chapter I'll explain:
- ✓ How to win and delight your first customers.
- ✓ How to build a customer experience that scales.
- ✓ How to turn delighted customers into social proof.

Step 1: Win and delight your first customers

A customer only commits if he trusts your brand.

She needs to trust that:
- ✓ You fulfill your (contractual) promises, spoken or unspoken.
- ✓ You offer help when it's needed, and won't hide after the bill is paid.
- ✓ You are in it for the long haul.

Now as you are building your brand, you need to gain this trust. You need to convince them you have their best interest in mind. And this takes time.

So before anything, you need to convince people one at the time. Since you don't have a sales force (yet), this is often done by the founders.

Founders need to lend their personal credibility to get the first sales.

They are basically saying *"you can trust me to take care of you"*. This works better if said by the owner of the company instead of an employee, who has no skin in the game and could be gone tomorrow.

Paul Graham, the founder of Y Combinator writes:

"You should take extraordinary measures not just to acquire users, but also to make them happy."

This means a lot of personal visits, thank-you cards, service calls, gifts or dinners in order to convince your customer that their well-being is important to you.

You are both the founder, the salesman and the account manager – and totally infatuated by your first customers.

This helps a lot. Graham writes: *"You can delight a customer with an early, incomplete and buggy product if you make up the difference with attentiveness."*

Don't worry about the scalability of your efforts yet.

Yes, treating your first customers like your first girlfriend (or boyfriend) costs time, money and energy. It'll be a full-time job as the brand grows.

But now you are building something. With growth, scalability will be a champagne problem. Besides:

Delighting customers scales better than you expect.

Thank-you notes can be written in between orders, staff can be trained, things can be automated. For now:

Capture the experience of your very first customers in glowing reviews.

Explicitly ask them for it. If they were delighted, they will help. Then publish the review, including their full name, photo, title and company name/logo.

Step 2: Create a scalable customer experience

To create an experience that delights your customer,

A. List all the moments you are in contact with them.

Perhaps you can add some.

B. Then see how you can go the extra mile.

For Toby, we came up with some good ones worth sharing:
- Add hand-written, personal thank-you notes to most deliveries.
- A chat widget on the site that was staffed around the clock.
- Asking customers for photos of their dog, showcasing them online and on social media as "Friends".
- Our CEO calls the customers themselves, and send a custom follow-up mail afterward.
- Our veterinarian answers questions which are health-related, giving customers a free vet-on-demand.
- A "Make Us Better" form that encourages customers to deposit their ideas on improving our product and service.
- Free treats at the dog's birthday, which often gets neglected in the household.
- Toby-branded dog gifts and gave them away at 3, 6 and 12 months of membership, and every year after that.
- Donations in customers names to a relevant charity (Animal Ambulance) and let them know with a personal email.
- Our in-house veterinarian answers frequently asked questions and others with video in a lab coat.
- A conversational tone in all correspondence, on social media and emails.

C. Figure out the costs per idea in money and handling time for each idea.

Personalizing your welcoming emails doesn't cost you any money, but sending gifts does. So even though I encourage you to go the extra mile, your efforts should be sustainable.

Of course, we searched for ways to unburden ourselves whilst delivering great service. Most actions were standardized, scheduled or automated.

Step 3: Turn delighted customers into social proof

Good reviews help build trust.

By giving you a good review, a customer ties their name to your brand. Their credibility is now added to yours.

The more reviews, the more trust, the easier the conversion.

For Toby, we decided to collect our reviews via Trustpilot. Two weeks after we sent our first package, our customer receives an email from Trustpilot: "Review Toby and win!"

A. Incentivize users (1) to leave reviews and (2) to be extra thankful.

For B2C, use incentives to generate (good) testimonials for your site and on review platforms like use Trustpilot, Google Reviews or similar services.

We raffle free dog food every week and users leave wonderful reviews. They somehow think that criticism won't help their raffle.

B. Always respond to reviews, especially the critical ones.

If customers see that your business values reviews, they leave one more easily. Plus, you might be able to seduce the critical ones to reduce or drop their negativity.

C. Give people their money back when they ask for it.

If people feel they spend their money wrongly, they will bitch about you online. Most of the time, the dollars ain't worth the negativity.

For businesses, you've got to pull favors.

No sane purchase manager is going to give you a glowing review for the chance to win a little dogfood. You've got to speak to the relationship and ask for a favor.

After they gave the review, ask for them to paste in on the platforms like Capterra, G2Crowd. If these aren't relevant, Google Reviews will do fine.

Summary and steps for servicing your customers

Delighted customers purchase more and more often, refer their friends and leave you wonderful reviews.

- ☑ Step 1: Win and delight your first customers
- ☑ Step 2: Create a scalable customer experience
    - A. List all the moments you are in contact with them.
    - B. hen see how you can go the extra mile.
    - C. Figure out the costs per idea in money and handling time.
- ☑ Step 3: Turn delighted customers into social proof
    - A. Incentivize users (1) to leave reviews and (2) to be extra thankful.
    - B. Always respond to reviews, especially the critical ones.
    - C. Give people their money back when they ask for it.

6.5. How to create video content

"Film is a matter of what's in the frame and what's out."

Martin Scorsese

Very few people like reading. For the vast majority, it's hard and tedious labor. They much rather watch a video.

Video is your audience's favorite way to absorb information.[18]

A Facebook executive predicted the platform will be all video, adding that video is "the best way to tell stories in this world" and "helps us to digest much more information."[19]

Luckily, you as a brand builder can profit from this trend. For what better way to communicate your brand promise than through video?

Making video's is easier than ever - you can shoot and edit 4K video on your mobile phone.

And to a certain extent, crummy production value only adds to your video's authenticity and realism.

In this chapter we'll explore:
- ✓ How to make viral videos.
- ✓ Steps for creating a video.

"Sooo much better than the book I didn't read..."

How to make viral videos

The wet dream of every brand builder is a video being spread around the world for free. This is very rare, but you can increase the odds.

Any video can go viral if your audience keeps sharing it in their network. But they'll do this only when your video evokes intense emotion.

We're talking about serious doses of awe, joy, hope, nostalgia or sympathy. Perhaps some anger.

This is why animations hardly go viral – it's hard to inspire the above emotions with cartoons. Also, some video ingredients are better at evoking emotion than others.

Old people, babies, and animals inspire emotion the easiest.

"Awesome."

Your brand shouldn't be the center stage in the video. People won't spread a story tainted by an overt commercial motive. At best the video is allowed to portray the emotional impact of your product or service.

Step 1: Define the purpose and type of your video

You can't expect your video to be effective without a clear purpose. It decides the type, length, and location of your videos.

Don't just start yapping into the camera. Settle on a purpose first.

"My commute was like - crazy - you guys...."

The questions below should give you some direction where to start.

A: Decide in what stage to show the video.

Before you pick a video type, you must know the patience and comprehension level of your audience when they see your video.

Awareness stage
- Your audience is unaware of you and perhaps unaware of their problem.
- They'll have no patience and no understanding. Keep it short and simple.
- Examples are your home page, landing pages or social media profiles.

Consideration stage
- Your audience understands their problem and is exploring your solution.
- They are willing to watch longer and more complex videos.
- Example locations are your product and about pages.

Decision stage
- Your audience wants to fix their problem and is researching brands.
- They are willing to watch longer and more complex videos.
- Example locations are the testimonial and conversion pages.

Loyalty stage

- Your committed audience is starting to experience your brand benefits.
- Now you can hit them with the long-form video content.
- Example locations are your emails, knowledge base and news feed.

You can use video in each stage.

Pick a video type and purpose.

You must now pick a type of video and purpose. They must fit the stage you're showing it in.

Pitch videos
- A pitch video describes a problem and offers your brand as a solution. It often describes a fictional buyer who gets his need solved.
- Purpose: evoke the need for your brand in your audience.
- Format for SaaS: Animation. Complex software needs simplicity.
- Format for others: Video. It inspires emotion the easiest.
- Length estimate: 30 to 60 seconds.
- Suitable for stage: awareness.

Story video
- A story video describes a situation where a protagonist interacts with your brand and shows positive emotion as they reap the results.
- Purpose: tie a positive emotion to your brand.
- Format: video.
- Length estimate: 20 to 90 seconds.
- Suitable for stage: awareness, consideration, decision, loyalty.

Brand videos
- A brand video showcases your organization and its grand ambitions. The mission & vision, working culture and history can be addressed.
- Purpose: convince the audience your organization shares their values.
- Format: live video.
- Length estimate: 1 to 5 minutes.
- Suitable for stage: consideration, decision.

Interview videos

- Interview videos put experts in your brand's field in front of the camera to answer interesting questions.
- Purpose: inspire trust and build authority with your audience.
- Format: Video.
- Length estimate: 1 to 60 minutes.
- Suitable for stage: consideration, decision, loyalty

Event videos

- Event videos show highlights of what your audience can expect at your conference, fundraiser or trade mart.
- Purpose: interest your audience for a visit.
- Format: Video.
- Length estimate: 20 to 60 seconds.
- Suitable for stage: awareness, consideration, decision, loyalty

Case study videos

- A case study video portrays satisfied customers who describe how your brand helped them achieve their goals.
- Purpose: convince the audience your brand can fulfill the promise.
- Format: Video.
- Length estimate: 30 to 120 seconds.
- Suitable for stage: decision

Educational videos

- Educational videos teach your audience something new.
- Purpose: build authority and a following as you educate your audience about things relevant to your brand.
- Format: Video, animation, or a combination.
- Length estimate: 3 to 30 minutes.
- Suitable for stage: awareness, consideration, decision, loyalty

Have you got a video type and purpose in mind? Good, write it down.

Perhaps yours is a hybrid of the above. No matter. Just make sure you write down the purpose, format, and length of whatever you want.

Step 2: Choose who's going to make your video

You've now got a video to produce. But there is too much competition for it to suck. Your audience will instantly dismiss videos that ain't worth their time - and they can smell junk like a bloodhound on cocaine.

Woofie will be fine.
It's (mostly) baking soda.

Option I: Hire a creative agency.

They will do scripting, production, and editing for you. This can be expensive.

Option II: Hire a production company or freelancer.

The name gives it away: they bring some gear and shoot some material for you. You must script, edit and often direct. This is cheaper but leaves a lot of creative freedom with you.

Option III: Do it yourself.

You do everything yourself.

Step 3: Write a video script

Every great video starts with a clearly articulated script. Even those without strict choreography – like interviews and case studies – should be prepared with (follow-up) questions.

A. To kickstart yourself, dig up some inspiration.

Check out the videos of analogous brands, and study them from beginning to end. See what they do right, and take note.

B. Brainstorm for rough outlines.

Now it's time to sketch the outline for your video. Brainstorm alone or with colleagues about what theme, emotion or solution your video will highlight.

Some questions that may help:
- What emotion should our brand inspire?
- What benefit do you want to convey at a minimum?
- What protagonist will my audience identify with?
- What situations does the audience face?
- Does this outline fit within the constraints of the Brand Identity?

C. Condense your outlines into a script that fits the timeframe.

The script is nothing more than 3 columns, describing (1) when your audience (2) sees and (3) hears things. Don't worry, you're not trying to get Martin Scorsese to frame it on his bedroom wall. Just get the idea on paper.

"Shouldn't have wasted my time in cinema."

Don't forget to have a strong opener (hook) and close with a call to action that tells people to try your brand or visit your store.

D. Subject your script to criticism.

First, ask yourself the hard questions:
- If you act the script out, does it still feel right?
- If you articulate all the text, does it still fit within the time frame?
- Would you watch this video all the way through if it wasn't yours?

If you answer 'yes' to these questions, you are ready to:

Ask your colleagues, clients, and audience to critize the script.

You don't want to get stoned by your stakeholders once the editing is done. It will be too late to salvage your video.

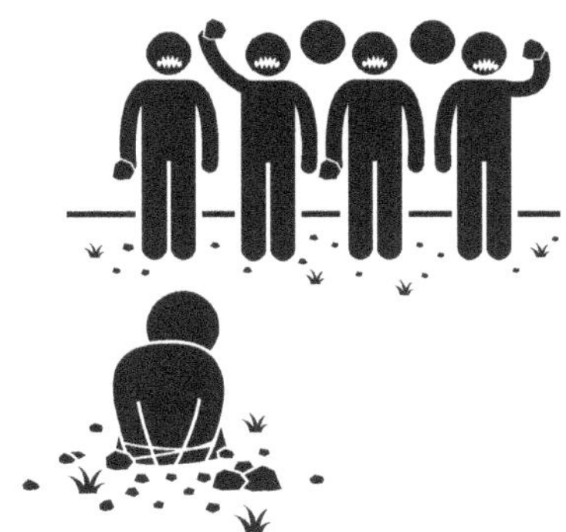

"It doesn't have any viral potential!"

Start shooting if everything goes well. If not, go back to the drawing board.

Step 4A: Shoot your video

Shooting video can be done with any prosumer camera. Whatever script or setting you choose, the following three ingredients will magnify your production value:

- **Proper light.** Shoot outdoors, or use a naturally lit room. Artificial light can fail to deliver if you don't have a competent crew shooting for you.
- **Crisp audio.** Your video will suffer greatly from crackly recordings, hauling wind or a speaker who sounds like he's locked in a flotation tank. Use an external microphone instead of your camera's.
- **Depth of field.** This means your subject is in focus (sharp) and the background isn't. It requires a serious camera and some practice, but the result is worth it.

Can't shoot a scene because of budget or time constraints? Browse for stock video ⬤ that might complement your own footage.

Step 4B: Animate your video

Animation can be extremely labor-intensive. This makes it expensive to produce unless you're willing to invest weeks yourself.

I buy animation or explainer kits online ⬤. Then I animate by clicking together scenes. The promo video for this book was made with one.

If you hand a freelancer skilled in After Effects both the animation kit and the script you should be able to procure your video within a limited budget.

You can also buy HUD elements, animated graphs, and other resources to overlay on your live video.

Step 5: Edit your video

Video editing is easy – you drag pieces of footage across a timeline until it flows. I use After Effects and Premiere, but there are (free) alternatives.

A. Settle on music, voice-over and sound effects first.

This allows you to coincide visuals and sounds. A video that synchronizes music, voice and video is exponentially more powerful.

"OK, but now beatbox *as* you somersault."

You can source stock music and sound effects online ✎.

Voiceovers can be done by freelancers www.fiverr.com www.freelancer.com. Don't forget to ask for their portfolio and a sample first. Compare their price to others before you commit.

If your voice-over is not in yet – just dub it yourself. You can replace it later with the real thing.

B. Source an editing template. (Optional)

There's a shortcut to impressive editing: you can use templates. These are ready-made video files: you insert your footage and render an impressive production.

Search for "After Effects Templates" and get inspired ✎.

Why not add some serious shine with a logo animation? It will add power to your call to action – and credibility and coolness to the entire video.

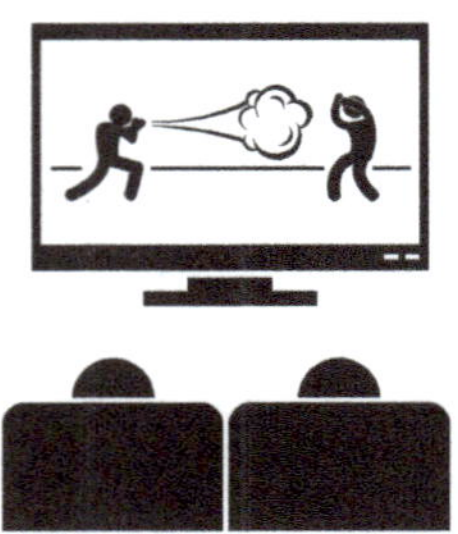

Online there are loads of templates that will accommodate your logo with a few clicks, churning out a professional result for a few bucks.

Search for "Logo Animation Template" 🔧.

These often include instructions on how to work the template. Can't figure it out? Ask either the creator or a freelancer skilled in After Effects to insert your logo.

Step 7: Publish your video

I prefer hosting video at a specialized platform like YouTube over a custom player on my site for three reasons:
1. Video is bulky and can eat into your server capacity.
2. Browsers on every device handle YouTube video players well.
3. The video can attract a bit of the YouTube audience.

So upload your video to YouTube or Vimeo and embed it into your website. If you are using a paid video platform that allows for extra analytics, adjust your privacy policy.

Summary and steps to create video content for your brand

Video is your audience's favorite way to absorb information. It helps them to digest much more information.

You must decide on the purpose, type, length and deployment location of each video, accounting for the patience and comprehension level of your audience.

Videos should be produced following a clear process, or they tend to suck. And they only go viral if it evokes intense emotion.

- ☑ Step 1: Define the purpose and type of your video.
- ☑ Step 2: Choose who's going to make your video.
  Option I: Hire a creative agency.
  Option II: Hire a production company or freelancer.
  Option III: Do it yourself.
- ☑ Step 3: Write a video script.
  A. To kickstart yourself, dig up some inspiration.
  B. Brainstorm for rough outlines.
  C. Condense your outlines into a script that fits the timeframe.
  D. Subject your script to criticism.
- ☑ Step 4: Shoot or animate your video.
- ☑ Step 5: Edit your video.
  A. Settle on music, voice-over and sound effects first.
  B. Source an editing template (Optional)
- ☑ Step 6: Add a logo animation (Optional)

6.6. How to build a social media following

"When you say it, it's marketing. When they say it, it's social proof."

Andy Crestodina

I don't use social media much. They leech your data, allow others to profile you and cloak the entire parasitic charade in comfy language. Yuck.

"Our mission is to give people the power to build community
and bring the world closer together."

However, most people use social media. Including your audience.

Soccer moms are on Facebook, journalists on Twitter. Heck, even grouches like me use LinkedIn! So build a following for your brand on these platforms.

Social media is a versatile and cost-effective way to reach your audience.

Besides the obvious benefits to you, people expect serious brands to have a serious social media presence.

But you can't just drop a post and walk away. That's just online autism.

Doing it wrong will hurt you, for even social media junkies somehow consider their time valuable, and won't allow you to waste it.

Yet doing it well may cost serious resources. The return on investment can be uncertain. And you probably don't feel like it.

I'll explain how to do it well in a time and cost-effective manner.

I'll cover:
- ✓ Rules for social media
- ✓ How to choose the right social media networks
- ✓ How to set up your brand on social media
- ✓ How to build a following
- ✓ How to engage with your following

It will be fun.

But if you're still unwilling to do social media afterwards, delegate it.

For this chapter you can download the Social Media Content Worksheet 🔧.

Rules for social media

Let's start with the dynamics of social media. It's a strange but magical place where a semi-anonymous herd gets to act on their most primitive impulses.

But perhaps we can bend them to our advantage.

It's a hard crowd to please.

In the online public forum, individuals have little to lose.

They're safe and (relative) anonymous. If they don't veer into death threats, they're safe from legal and bodily harm.
Your brand, however, has everything to lose. All interaction is there for eternity, to be scrutinized, shared and ridiculed by others.

This dynamic has the following implications:
1. People know you have to be polite, despite their own rough behavior. This makes them skeptical of your kindness.
2. People know complaints must be resolved, regardless of their nature. This makes them eager to voice complaints publicly.

In short: the online crowd is hard to please.

"How can I be of service?

[User is typing]

Your social media audience wants authentic politeness.

Whether they come to complain, compliment or just hang out, they expect a warm welcome from a real human being. Everyone hates the scripted automatons that only pretend to give a sh*t.

Behave like an ambassador from a lesser power at a UN cocktail party.

Always be the last person to leave. Rub every shoulder that's willing. Politely deflect verbal assaults. Never lose your composure.

And if you go after someone, do it with family-friendly humor.

"haha…. excuse me?"

If it suits your brand, you can play a bit rougher. Destroying your followers verbally can be a great crowd pleaser, albeit risky.

Always be principled. Draw a firm line with the undesirables.

Unfunny verbal abuse should be reprimanded like a grandfather would a naughty dog – friendly – perhaps humorously - but firm. There's no reason to let them tee off on you.

Unreasonable complaints should be kindly referred to your terms of service. If these are generous enough, you can stand your ground without looking like a prick.

Using social media means listening to your audience.

This is sometimes fun, often uncomfortable, but always instructive. As we saw, people don't mince words in relative anonymity.

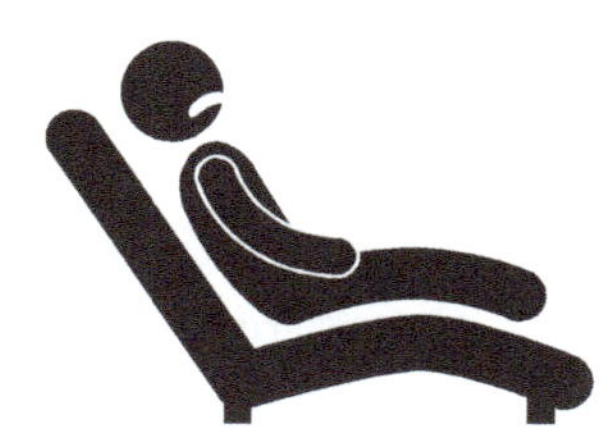

"Your brand is a total crock of sh*t. You will all burn in hell."

"I wish you'd tell me how you really feel..."

Users will be brutally honest in their assessment of you.

You'll find out:
- ✓ What language works, and what doesn't.
- ✓ Who loves your brand, and who detests it.
- ✓ What people find confusing about your brand.
- ✓ Why the brand promise doesn't sway certain audience members.
- ✓ What the weakest points are in your product or service.

Don't worry, you'll be entertained as well. Plenty of obscenities will be articulated without proper spelling, grammar or interpunction. Enjoy them.

"There are some things money just can't buy."

Truly social people give unscripted answers. They're willing to engage in meaningful conversations with strangers. They see being social as a good in itself.

It only works with a truly social attitude.

That's why the young are so good at it. They don't resent their paycheck (yet) and joyfully engage with your audience in the name of your brand.

Social media shouldn't be touched by cynics.

The wage-slave getting tasks to justify his presence shouldn't represent your brand. That's like sending your grumpy uncle to the door to greet your wedding guests because you're too busy.

Only give the passwords to those you'd hang out with yourself.

Social media is a perpetual commitment

You have to keep posting fresh content. It damages your brand if the last post is 6 months old – and was only liked by the founder's mother.

Like.

For every language on every platform, you will have to:
- Frequently post content that deserves attention.
- Engage with followers that comment and share your content.

If you can't manage this – don't start. Or shut down your page.

Step 1: Choose the right social media platforms

It's impossible to have a presence on all the social media platforms. You should select the platforms that your audience uses – and keep your focus on them.

A. Find out where your audience hangs out.

There are several methods to locate them:
- ✓ Check ⦿ which platform demogrpahics match those of your audience.
- ✓ Ask your audience directly what platforms they use.
- ✓ Use tools ⦿ that show who hangs out where by analysing social data.
- ✓ Look at the social media strategy of similar brands.

B. Make sure you have the skills to produce content for your platform.

To create quality content, you'll need to be adept with images, video, or copywriting. YouTube requires high-quality video content. Instagram and Pinterest use great-looking images.

You probably have a shortlist of candidates by now. Rank them according to their potential.

C. Claim every handle on the shortlist.

Usernames are called handles. Your audience finds your handle by searching for your brand name, so *always* include your full brand name in your handle.

If possible, try to use the same handle across all your platforms. Use tools ⦿ to check if your handles are available. If it's unavailable, add 'official', 'real' or something more creative. (OriginalJuicyCow)

You should register a handle for each social media platform on your shortlist. Even if you aren't using them now. It prevents competitors, clowns, and cat-ladies from claiming your space.

D. Choose one or two platforms to start with.

If you're building a brand, it's likely your resources are limited. Some founder will be doing the social media as a side-project, or interns take turns running it.

That's why you'll want to start with one or two platforms. It allows you to invest in quality content and frequent responses.

Check your shortlist and decide which platforms (1) align with your goals, (2) have the biggest user base and (2) are most likely to yield a good return on investment.

E. Set up multilingual pages for your platforms. (Optional)

Be wary of using English if (a chunk of) your audience is German. They might speak both, but there are barriers to being social in a non-native language.

That's why brands serving multiple countries can set up a (1) global page) and (2) a page for each local language. Imagine 'JuicyCow' is your global handle. It's in English, as it serves everybody around the globe.

Now for each local market, you can register a handle with the country code behind it: 'JuicyCowDE' for Germany or 'JuicyCowJP' for Japan.

"Oaidekite ureshi desu, JuicyCow!"

Be careful. It is not merely a matter of translating content. You'll have to engage your following in their language as well.

Only bigger brands bother with a page for every market they serve. They have minions to produce content and replies in each language.

Step 2: Set up your pages

Congratulations. You've chosen your social media platforms and claimed the handles. You're now ready to set up your pages.

A. Insert your information.

Your page should include a short pitch so newcomers know what your brand is about. Keep it short and sweet, or just use your war cry.

Always include a clickable call to action to convert your following. Social media should yield results, and followers must be able to commit somehow.

B. Insert your graphics.

The logo and cover graphics have specific lengths and widths on each platform. Find these dimensions and tailor your graphics accordingly.

Better still are templates ⊘. They show the dimensions, but also which areas are visible on each screen size.

Your cover grabs the most attention, so be sure to use an image that conveys your brand promise. Decorate it with text if it pleases you.

C. Ask your network to follow you.

The first 25 followers serve as proof that your page is worth following. No-one will like a page that no-one else likes.

The easiest way to kickstart this following is to ask your network to like you. This causes queasy feelings, as you're (hopefully) not used to begging for approval.

I know it feels queesy, but just bite through it.

For the best results, avoid the automated requests your people are flooded with. Send an authentic personal message instead. It makes it harder to ignore your request:

"Hey [name]! After gallons of sweat, blood, and tears, I finally got around to realizing my dream of building [brand]. I'd love to keep you posted, so you'd do me a favor by hitting the 'follow' button here [page link]. It won't be spammy - promise. Thanks already!"

D. Integrate tracking mechanisms on your website. (Optional)

Most platforms provide a piece of code tracking the platform's users as they interact with your website and ads.

These cookies allow you to track conversions from ads, define audiences for future ads, and remarket to people who have interacted with your website.

If you're using this technology, you can use the platform's documentation or other manuals to build it into your website.

Update your privacy policy accordingly. These cookies are pretty invasive and exposure user behaviour.

I said *behaviour.*

Each page needs followers who like, share, click or comment on the content. If a post gathers a lot of these 'engagements', the platform will label it as valuable. It will show up in more user feeds.

So the larger your following, the more potential engagement, the bigger the reach of your brand.

But how to get people to click 'follow'? How to make them care? What if you can't feature panda videos? The answer is surprisingly simple, yet demanding to execute.

A. List the subjects your audience cares about.

The secret to building a following is posting content that is useful to your audience.

They scroll through mountains of nonsense on a daily basis. Your posts should deliver that rare piece of entertainment or knowledge.

If your post evokes an emotional response, even better. Laughs, cries, empathy and especially outrage have users press the 'like' button like a famished Pavlovian dog.

Conversely, your post about Friday's drinks might not do much. You can use these things as filler, but each sh*tty post is a reason to unfollow.

So make a list of subjects your audience actually cares about:
- ✓ See what similar brands serve up for content.
- ✓ Check the content of other pages they follow.
- ✓ Use tools to 🔧 analyze the interests of a defined audience.

Now you've got a list that will serve as inspiration for your own content. You can make sure it's accurate by asking your audience 🔧.

B. Build a process to source, process and publish content.

You should standardize the way you source, process and publish content. This makes Social Media easy to do and delegate.

i. Download the Social Media Content Worksheet.

ii. Structure how you source content.

With a structure you can create a steady stream of content. Examples:
- Gather company news like product updates, vacancies and behind the scenes stories.
- Gather content from your users. Interview them, ask for reviews, ask for pictures. They love to be highlighted, but you can further incentivize them with contests.
- Use tools to collect the content of relevant sites, accounts, and influencers writing about the subjects on your list.
- Use tools to generate content ideas based on your subject list.

iii. List the steps and tools for processing and posting content.

With a list of steps, you reduce errors and increase speed. For example:
- Check each post for spelling and plagiarism.
- Repost 3d party content with tools that add your branded links.
- Optimize for search engines by inserting keywords.

iv. Create a specific posting schedule.

Post too little and your audience will forget about you. Post too much and your engagements drop off, plus you annoy people for congesting their feed.

As for when to post: make sure your audience is on their feed when you do. You'll have more eyeballs, hence more engagement and reach.

Studies suggest the following frequencies and times:

	Minimum	Suggested	Maximum	Time
Facebook	3 x per week	1 x per day	2 x per day	Before 6:30 AM After 8:30 PM
LinkedIn	2 x per week	1 x per day	1 x per day	7:30 AM to 8:30 AM 12:00 PM 5:00 to 6:00 PM Tuesdays to Thursdays
Twitter	1 x per day	3 x per day	5 x per day	12:00 to 3:00 PM Mondays to Fridays
Instagram	1 x per day	1 x per day	3 x per day	Anytime except between 3:00 and 4:00 PM
Pinterest	3 x per day	5 x per day	30 x per day	6:30 to 11:30 AM on weekdays 8:00 – 11:00 PM on weekends

C. Spend money to get your content in front of your audience. (Optional)

If users see your content for free, the platform itself isn't making any money. This is why commercial content can be deprioritized in the user feed. It gives you an incentive to 'promote' your post, in other words: to pay for eyeballs.

This makes organic growth harder. To build a following and keep your posts in front of them, you'll probably need to spend some money. It prevents a post from dying after your mother hit the like button.

Every platform has different ways to do this. Run an experiment and see if the added engagement is worth your cash.

Step 4: Engage with your following

Perhaps you know the dopamine kick that a bunch of likes delivers. It's an awesome feeling – signaling that people think you and your content are valuable.

Any like, comment or share is called an 'engagement'.

Only a small percentage of your following engage with each post. If you do not respond to their efforts, they will feel ignored.

Don't ignore followers. They'll disengage from your content and brand.

Even though you need to respond to all sane and less sane engagements, you don't want to spend all day doing it.

But don't automate your responses. Or regurgitate the standard 'thank you' whenever someone shares or comments. Followers can smell fake and will disengage as if you'd ignored them. No:

You'll need to respond efficiently *and* authentically to each engagement.

That's of course, a tender balance.

Here are some ways to increase the efficiency of your replies:
- ✓ **Use tools.** Some tools ⚙ gather all your social media engagements and messages in a single inbox, using (push)notifications when you need to reply.
- ✓ **Block your social media time.** Make sure you're not constantly responding. Schedule one or two blocks of half an hour each.
- ✓ **Script responses.** By saving answers to frequently asked questions you can speed up your responses. Craft several so you don't look like a robot.
- ✓ **Make a folder of GIF's.** You can download some GIF's that say 'thank you', 'awesome', or 'well done'. ⚙ Just paste them from your folder into the reply.

Here are some ways to increase the authenticity of your replies:

- ✓ **Add a name.** Sign each response with your (fictional) first name. Adding '– Jennifer' to each reply reminds the follower that he's interacting with real human beings – not just a faceless logo.
- ✓ **Use emojis.** They're the easiest way to add some humanity to your replies. Use them to convey the emotions that plain text lacks.
- ✓ **Use gifs.** Just like emojis, they have the power to spice up your text. And since there's a GIF for every social situation, it's easy to dig one up that fits your reply. They are also great for thanking followers without being smarmy.
- ✓ **Use images.** They're the fast way to answer questions. It saves you the typing, and the follower the reading. Go the extra mile by drawing personal messages on the screenshot.
- ✓ **Use video.** This might sound like an outrageous investment but a reply can be recorded in 10 seconds. It's experienced as extremely personal and is hence a sure-fire way to prove you actually care.
- ✓ **Ask questions.** How did they experience [insert topic blog post]? Do they agree with how you handled [insert anecdote]? If they respond, you can continue the conversation and build a relationship between that person and your brand.

Be sure to combine the efficiency tips with the above authenticity tips.

And if you can find it in your heart, try to have some fun. Social media is a miraculous playground. You can engage with the world from a piece of glass in your hand.

"Let's just enjoy the miracle, you guys!"

Summary and steps for building a social media following

Most people are on social media. It's a versatile and cost-effective way to reach your audience.

Yet the online crowd is hard to please. Their relative anonymity makes them brutally honest, skeptical of kindness and eager to voice complaints publicly. Be authentically polite, yet draw a firm line with the undesirables.

Social media only works if you're sociable. It has to be kept alive with regular fresh content. If you can't manage this – don't start.

- ☑ Step 1: Choose the right social media networks:
    - A. Find out where your audience hangs out.
    - B. Make sure the platform functionality matches your goals.
    - C. Make sure you have the skills to produce content for your platform.
    - D. Choose one to three platforms to start with.
- ☑ Step 2: Set up your brand on social media:
    - A. Create a branded company page on each chosen platforms:
        - i. Is your brand name unavailable? Add prefixes.
        - ii. Design your cover photos and banners using templates.
        - iii. Create company pages for each local market you serve. [Optional]
    - B. Claim the company handle on each platform you plan on using.
- ☑ Step 3: Build a following:
    - A. Find out what your audience considers valuable content.
    - B. Create a process for sourcing, editing, and publishing content:
        - i. Make sure it is easy to understand and easy to delegate.
        - ii. Use tools to manage publishing. [Optional]
        - iii. Recruit colleagues and friends to engage . [Optional]
        - iv. Pay to boost your content. [Optional]
    - C. Execute as you track your engagement and follows.
- ☑ Step 4: Engage with your following

6.7. How to get pixel-perfect print design

"Caress the detail, the divine detail."

Vladimir Nabokov

You may suspect that the age of print is over. Digital things are cheap, have great exposure potential and are mighty convenient.

However, old school folk have powerful arguments for printing stuff:
- ✓ **Print is physical.** Proposals and brochures stick to the desk of your prospect, while their digital stuff is easily deleted or lost.
- ✓ **Print gives legitimacy.** Printed things feel timeless and full of authority. A physical brochure just feels more serious than a digital one.
- ✓ **Print is engaging.** It feels natural to skim a digital document, just as it feels natural to study a physical one.

Also, digital brochures and flyers are very handy. Your potential customer can review it at their leisure, or share it with colleagues and family.

I'll explain how to do it right in a time and cost-effective manner.

Let's cover:
- ✓ Rules for print
- ✓ How to choose a format
- ✓ How to select your elements
- ✓ How to source a design
- ✓ How to proof & print

Rules for print

Designing for print requires prudence. Mistakes are expensive because you need to re-print everything. It also causes delays. So there will be a scapegoat when a batch is botched:

"Did you fail to convert to CMYK?"

To make sure the finger points elsewhere, let's identify some rules. They prevents most quality errors and delays.

Make sure every image has the right resolution

Low-resolution images will ruin your print run. The design feels amateurish if you can identify the individual pixels on an image.

Every image must have 300 dpi (dots per inch) at the size you're printing.

Typical web resolution is only 72 dpi, so those Googled images can only be used at 1/4th their size. Your computer can measure the dpi of your images.

Make sure all your images have the right resolution for their output size.

If you insist on using a blurry picture, there are online tools ⊘ that enhance colors and increase resolution.

Woofie looks more friendly in low resolution for some reason.

Most design work is done in Red, Green, and Blue. RGB gives extremely precise control and allows for almost 17 million colors.

However, no professional printer on this planet uses RGB. They define colors with Cyan, Magenta, Yellow and Key/Black (CMYK).

Why is that? Because a monitor displays color with light, where print displays colors with ink. That's why CMYK has a smaller color gamut (reach) than RGB.

Printers convert RGB pictures and illustrations to CMYK. This replaces every out-of-gamut color. Needless to say, the result can disappoint because you can end up with radically different colors.

"Which RGB designing brand builder
just got himself fired?"

Set the color mode to CMYK in your design tool before you start.

This limits your design to colors that can actually be printed and avoids unpleasant surprises.

Documents are often printed together on a large sheet of paper, then trimmed to size. This trimming requires every design to have space beyond the actual dimensions, commonly known as the bleed area.

Add 6mm to the width and height of your designto get the standard 3mm bleed.

Crop marks show where the design ends and the bleed begins. It's where the knife is put when the trimming starts.

Add crop marks to identify the trim lines on your document.

Finally, you should add margins around your design (at least 10 mm) to make sure your design elements don't look like they're falling off the page.

Add margins to give your design elements the space they need.

Always set the bleed areas (green), crop marks (red) and margins (blue) before you start designing to ensure your design can be printed correctly. Most design tools can add these for you.

Step 1: Choose your format, size, and materials

Every piece of print, from brochures to packaging, comes with options:

> **Format:** The concept of the print – like folded versus normal business cards. If it can be imagined, it can probably be printed.
> **Size:** The dimensions of the paper – like A4 vs A5 brochures. Small is easily carried, large accommodate more stuff.
> **Materials:** The weight, texture, and finish of the material - like shine versus no-shine. Most printers send (white-labeled) samples on request.

A. Choose what (1) can contain your info, (2) suits your brand and (3) fits your budget.

The majority of brands play it safe. They use regular formats, sizes and paper types. You'll easily stand out if you deviate from the standard.

"He'll never forget my 55" solid glass business card."

But while exotic print catches the eye, it's more expensive. And anything outside of A4 often has to be redesigned for PDF. When you've chosen:

B. Write down the dimensions of the required design, including the bleeds.

Or better yet, download the templates for your design software that your printer offers. These will save you a lot of headaches.

Step 2: List the elements and sketch the layout

Before investing in design, sketch a coarse layout first.

Start by listing all the elements you want to include in your design. Next, arrange them across the pages. You can use pen and paper or PowerPoint.

Try to be creative. Images can start on one page and continue on the other. Or make the headers complementary. Reading your print will be a tiny adventure if you're creative enough with the layout.

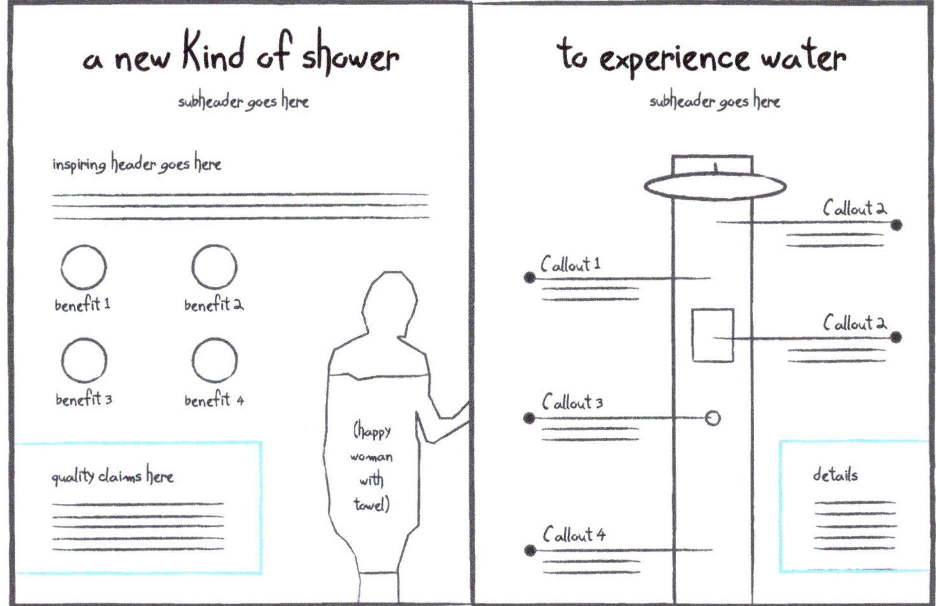

The information density depends on the purpose of your print and your audience.

Always check how similar brands do it. Car brochures often contain multiple sheets of data that no-one reads but serve as authoritative stuffing. Lingerie billboards go with just some disrobed women and the brand's logo.

Stuck? Try digging up some inspiration on Pinterest. It contains countless unique billboards, brochures, and business cards.

Step 3: Source your design

There are several ways to source your design, depending on your skills and budget:

Option 1: Design it yourself

Designing print is nothing more than putting the right elements in the right place. And Adobe InDesign - the leading software for this - isn't hard to use.

That said, designing something that tickles the imagination often takes years of experience. And getting it pixel-perfect requires time and multiple iterations.

Option 2: Pay someone ($100 - $2,000)

Designing is not a rare skill, hence designers are not as expensive as coders. However, you get what you pay for. Bottom-shelf designers rarely produce masterpieces.

When paying someone, be sure to complete step 1.

You can also include step 2 in the briefing. It eliminates surprises but limits creative freedom. You can also send some examples that you find inspiring.

Before you commit to a designer:
- ✓ Check her portfolio to ensure their quality matches your ambition.
- ✓ Check her reviews to see if she delivers on time and budget.
- ✓ Make sure the price includes multiple rounds of iterations.
- ✓ Get a clear deadline, and include some margin for iterations.
- ✓ Make sure the copyrights and original files are transferred afterward.

Check the online tools list ⊘ for where to find quality designers.

Option 3: Write out a competition. ($200 - $1.000)

There are websites ⊘ that host design competitions – from hoodies to packaging and book layouts. You can dismiss the designs you dislike and get new iterations on the ones you do.

Again: step 1, and if possible step 2 can be used as a briefing. However, the more detailed you are, the more you limit their creative freedom.

Put up more money to attract better designers.

Option 4: Get a template ($10 - $50)

There's a template for everything. Search for 'Brochure Template', and you'll find a lot of free and paid ones. I use them for inspiration only – inserting all your fonts, colors and images can be laborious – and the uniqueness is always minimal.

There are also online templating tools ⊘. Here, you can pick a design and drag-and-drop your content. No software or skills required.

Even my brother Bart can do it!

Step 4: Review and print

Many errors creep into your design, from spelling to structure. To eliminate nasty surprises, review the design before you print.

Export your design in PDF-X1a. It includes all print-related requirements.

A. Export your design to a digital PDF and check it.

- ✔ Inspect the photos and illustrations. Can anything use retouching?
- ✔ Check the spelling. If your design tool won't help, paste the text in a tool.
- ✔ Scan the last and first words in columns or pages for a correct flow.
- ✔ Are the headlines and text complete?
- ✔ Is the text consistently ragged (regular) or justified (touching the ends)?

B. Recruit fresh eyes to scan for errors.

The more time you spend with a design, the more invisible errors become. You should let others review your design to make sure it's faultless.

C. Get a proof from your printer. (Optional)

Never do expensive print runs without a proof. This is a sample that shows you how your design file looks look in real life.

A PDF won't do. Your monitor isn't reality, so the colors might turn out different in print. And don't use your desktop printer – the quality won't be representative. So ask your printer for a proof. Then check:

- ✔ Is the paper size and type right?
- ✔ How did the colors turn out?
- ✔ Are all the images and graphics razor-sharp?
- ✔ Are the outer and inner margins correct and consistent?
- ✔ Does the binding cut off or hide things?

For big products – like billboards - ask for a reduced-size proof or one showing only a critical piece.

D. Print and publish

Printing the double quantity is often only marginally more expensive than the printing the quantity you actually need.

Don't order more. You'll have to make the inevitable changes. And who wants to deal with pounds and pounds of obsolete paper?

For publishing *digital* documents I recommend to:

1. Export the design as an interactive PDF with links. Use the export options to keep your documents under 2 MB.
2. Rename it so it is easily searched for: "Brand Name Brochure EN"
3. Upload the document to your server or into your Wordpress CRM.
4. Create branded links that anaylse document traffic. (Optional)

OK, you can hit that send button now. Say a little prayer as you do.

Summary and steps for pixel-perfect print design

There are many advantages to print: it's physical, gives legitimacy and is engaging. Also, digital documents always come in handy.

Always make sure (1) your images have the right resolution, (2) you design in CMYK and (3) set the bleeds, crop marks, and margins before you start designing.

- ☑ Step 1: Choose the format:
    A. Choose the format, size, and materials that suit your purpose and budget.
    B. Write down the design dimensions and bleeds.
    Request a template from your printer (Optional).
- ☑ Step 2: List the elements and sketch the layout.
- ☑ Step 3: Source your design:
    Option 1: Design it yourself.
    Option 2: Pay someone. $100 - $2.000
    Option 3: Write out a competition. $200 - $1.000
    Option 4: Get a template. $10 - $50
- ☑ Step 4: Review and print:
    A. Export your design to a digital PDF and check it.
    B. Recruit fresh eyes to scan for errors.
    C. Get a proof from your printer. (Optional)
    D. Print and publish.

Save your work in a folder called "/brandname/print/project/".

6.8. How to build an email list

"Selling to people who actually want to hear from you is more effective than interrupting strangers who don't."

Seth Godin

Your email list is your gold mine. It contains the part of your audience that's genuinely interested in your brand, from prospects to loyal customers.

Building an email list has the following advantages:
- ✓ **Most people use email**: It beats social media and even search engines.
- ✓ **Permission-based:** Your email list contains only those who have chosen to be subjected to your stories.
- ✓ **Personalization:** You can personalize every email with user data.
- ✓ **Non-intrusive:** Your subscribers can open your email at their leisure.
- ✓ **Measurable:** Measure the success of each message and the interest of each subscriber.
- ✓ **Independent:** The list is yours. You're independent of platforms that can strip you from your following by booting or demonetizing you.

Of course, it's no cakewalk. You'll have to comply with privacy rules, deal with design and have the right forms, visuals, and segmentation in place.

Then each year, your list loses about 22% of email addresses because users switch companies, change email provider or simply opt-out. Your list growth should outpace this decay. We'll take a look at how.

Let's cover the rules for email and how to build and grow an email list

Let's get this goldmine going!

Let's start with the basics behind creating that goldmine for your brand.

Asking for an email is the easiest way to convert web traffic

About 70% of your website visitors never returns.

Why? They're on the internet, and there's a lot of stuff to do. If you're writing a blog, users read your things and leave. Or if you're selling shoes, users browse and bail.

It's just pretty hard to get an online sale or a donation from first-time visitors. That's a major commitment, something that requires your visitor to trust your brand.

That's why you try to get someone's email first.

It's a small first step. It's free and one can always unsubscribe.

The email address is then used to send (free) stuff that builds trust.

The more people open, read and click around your mails, the more space your brand gains in their mind. By feeding your prospects valuable things, they can grow into real customers ready to make real commitments.

"Eat up, now."

When you start out, no-one knows about you. But you'll meet a lot of people as you build your brand. And everyone is or knows a potential customer, donator, voter or investor.

Ask everyone you pitch if they'd like to be kept in the loop with the occasional email.

This might seem laborious, and a bit presumptuous, but this consolidates your encounter. The next time they open your mail, they'll remember your bright, hopeful face. Perhaps they'll even act on it – or forward it to a friend who might be interested.

Kickstart your list by converting every conversation.

Passionate pitchers
get things done.

The people you manually recruit will be amongst your most loyal subscribers.

When you land in someone's inbox, you enter their personal space. People can guard it fiercely, especially those who love empty inboxes.

Most people's inboxes are saturated with spammy, salesy emails. Don't add to this pile.

Only enter their email box when you've got something valuable to bring.

People hatcheting you (hitting the unsubscribe button) are statistically most likely to be annoyed with the volume of your irrelevant commercial drivel.

"Another one of those, huh?"

Ruthlessly judge the quality of your emails and list

The health of your email list can be derived from several statistics, each one tracked by every email marketing tool.

Your open rate shows how many recipients opened your email.

If those on your list are really interested in your brand, they are happy to receive your emails and will open them. If they don't open it, your emails are not expected to be interesting enough for them to bother. Try to add more value in the next ones.

Your click rate shows how many recipients clicked on at least one link in your email.

The goal of every email should be getting people to engage with your brand. That's why most people judge the success of a campaign by click rate.

If people aren't clicking on the articles, offers or links in your email, they are not interesting enough to explore further. Try to adjust the copy and content of your emails.

Your unsubscribe rate shows how many recipients asked to be 'unsubscribed'.

An unsubscribe means they judged your emails as unworthy of their time and attention. Try to find out why they left.

Did they leave shortly after signing up? Perhaps their expectations were off and you need to adjust your promises.

Did they leave after receiving commercial messages? Perhaps you need to rework them to be less intrusive or send them more free stuff before you pitch something.

Healthy lists have an open rate of 20%, a click rate of 3% and 0.25% unsubscribers per mail.

"That's where that sh*t goes."

Of course, this benchmark varies a bit per industry.

Stick to the law

Every country on earth has privacy and spam laws. If they don't, there's probably no email there either.

You have to follow the rules on privacy and spam.

This is easy because they're only a few of them. However, ignoring the rules can get you – in order of probability:

- Hatred from your audience;
- Booted from email platforms;
- Fined or persecuted by institutions.

Here's a list what you should and shouldn't do:

- ✓ Ask for permission: don't collect emails without consent.
- ✓ Write a privacy policy. Include at minimum:
  - A bullet list of data you collect from your audience.
  - What you are using this data for.
  - How people can review and change the data you have on them.
  - The effective date of the document.
- ✓ Only use the emails for the purposes as described in your privacy policy.
- ✓ Keep your email list secure. Use an established email marketing service.
- ✗ Do not web scrape emails – this is the practice of having a bot or a Bangladeshi scour the internet for leads and put the emails on your list.
- ✗ Do not use deceptive subject lines or header information.
- ✗ Do not sell your list or borrow it out. Don't buy or borrow one either.

If you're ever tempted to play cowboy with other people's data, think about Facebook. People breed permanent distrust with every shenanigan discovered.

Step 1: Select your email tool

You have many choices for email tools ⬨. Most are free to get start with.

A. Make sure your tool has all the functionality you need:

✓ Does the tool integrate with my CRM/Store? Are new customers pushed to the tool? Are open rates and click rates pushed to the CRM/Store?

✓ Can the tool send automated emails to new subscribers? This allows you to send a mini-course or other documents.

✓ You'll get more responses as your list grows. Is it able to send automated responses or convert customer responses into support tickets?

Got one? Well done!

B. Register for your tool of choice and complete its setup.

Step 2: Enable personalization and segmentation

Email tools offer personalization options.

This means including a first name or company name in the subject line of your mail, or in the body text. This makes the email feel more personal and relevant.

"Awww shucks... they thought of me..."

Email tools offer segmentation options, so you can target emails.

You can send an email to contact who match a certain condition, like language = English, or interest = press.

Naturally, both personalization and segmentation require you to add data to each contact in your list. I recommend adding the following where possible:

- First name
- Last name
- Company name
- Language
- Interest (With a dropdown: customer, investor, press)

A. Define the data for segmenting and personalization within your tool.

If you're building your list online, you shouldn't ask users for more than their first name and email address. It's just too much of a hassle.

Every form field causes friction. And friction destroys the conversion rate.

Once they become a real paying customer through your store or app, you can ask for the rest of your data. If you choose an email tool that integrates with your shop or CRM, new data points will be pushed to your list.

However, if you are getting users on the list manually, you can use a form asking for every data point you want.

B. For adding people to the list manually, design a form and save the URL.

Step 3: Define and produce an incentive.

No-one will just give you their email. You'll have to bribe them somehow.

"Here's a big fat bag of goodies for you.
Now if you'll just give me your email…"

A. Define an incentive to offer in exchange for a user's email.

Incentives convert best if they are:
- ✓ **Specific:** 'updates' or 'information' won't spark the imagination. Give them a real solution to a real problem they have.
- ✓ **Actionable:** Your incentive should provide a tool, checklist, skill or to-do list that the audience can easily and immediately apply.
- ✓ **Instantly accessible:** make sure your email tool sends it right away, or the website becomes instantly available.

Here are some examples:
- **Gated content.** Use a tool to lock website pages or a file. Their email unlocks it.
- **Premium content.** Enter your email to unlock exclusive content."
- **Giveaways.** Their email is used to send a free digital product, a discount code, or participate in a raffle. "Enter your email to win a dog house worth $500."
- **Create a quiz.** Create a quiz with a tool. Their email unlocks the result. "How agreeable are you in the office? Do our quiz and find out."
- **Mini-course.** Send your customers a series of emails that teaches them the essentials of a subject they care about. "Gardening Beginner's Course – learn the basics of gardening in 5 days."

B. Produce the incentive.

This means you write that eBook, design that infographic or buy that raffle gift. If it's a digital download, make sure to:

1. Export your document as an interactive PDF with links. Use the export options to keep your documents under 2 MB.
2. Rename it so it's easily searched for: "12 Tips for Self-Publishing.pdf"
3. Upload the document to your server or into your Wordpress CRM.
4. Use a tool 🔗 to create a link that analyses the traffic to the document. (Optional)
5. Create an automatic welcome for new subscribers in your email tool and include a link to your document.

Step 4: Deploy the opt-in form

By now you should know (1) the data you want from your customer, (2) what bribe you offer in exchange.

So when and how should you offer this deal?

At some point in your customer journey, you'll have to present them with a form where they can fill in their data.

Don't ask for their email too early.

They won't trust you with their email if you haven't been of value to them yet. So don't jam a popup in their face when they land on your site. You will have to calibrate the sweet spot.

Don't ask for their email too late.

If you wait to ask for 5 minutes on your websites, they might be gone by then. Or perhaps they're already warm enough to be nudged towards a real commitment instead of just giving an email.

"Just you wait for ONE GOSHDARN SECOND."

A. Pick the place and time to present your opt-in forms.

So when to present the form? And what method to use? Always empathize with your user – imagine their intent when they're browsing your site. You can use tools ✪ to observe this.

Be assertive enough to get those emails, but don't be pushy or annoying.

So pick the methods that rhyme with your audience and brand. As for what converts best, you can try different places and times.

- **In a popup.** The classic method is reviled and loved all over the internet. Darken the rest of the screen and put a bright form in their face.
- **In a landing page.** You can embed your form in a landing page - one that is built only for convincing your visitor to fill in that form.
- **In your email signature.** You can add a link in your email signature that goes to a form or a landing page.
- **Welcome gate.** Present the form immediately when they land on site.
- **Header or footer bars.** Add your form to the header and footer, or in a bar that stays with the user.
- **Upon leaving.** If you detect someone is about to close the tab, you can present the visitor with a popup.
- **In your blog post.** You can add the form in a sidebar or underneath each blog post, where users are most likely to be impressed by your knowledge.
- **Download pages.** Wherever people can get brochures, documents or other resources you can ask them for their email.
- **On request.** You can sprinkle links to your opt-in form throughout your content.

B. Choose a method to build and integrate your forms.

i. Use a tool that synchronizes with your email tool. They allow for everything described in this chapter, plus a whole lot more.
ii. Use the functionality of your email tool. Every email tool offers simple forms to embed in your site. No effort required, no result expected.
iii. Build it all yourself. If you resent using third-party tools, you can build the functionality you need yourself. Coding knowledge required.

C. Design an opt-in form that converts.

Never use crummy forms. Make sure they're well designed, blend with your website and use bright buttons.

They should contain at least:
- ✔ **A captivating headline.** The big benefit of giving you their email should be instantly clear.
- ✔ **A short description.** A few lines clarifying the headline. Don't forget to mention it's free.
- ✔ **Charming visuals.** Offering a free eBook? Add a mockup. A free course? Add a picture of the instructor looking at the form.
- ✔ **Descriptive button.** Never be creative in the text on your button. Buttons should describe exactly what happens: "Send me the eBook".

Remember to use as little form fields as possible. First name and email should be enough for now.

Summary and to-do for building an email list.

Because it's hard to get real commitment from first-time visitors, you ask for their email first. The email address is then used to send (free) stuff that builds trust.

Stick to the laws and keep judging the quality of your list using the open rate, click rate and unsubscribe rate.

- ☑ Step 1: Select your email tool:
    - A. Make sure it has all the functionality you need.
    - B. Register for your tool of choice and complete its setup.
- ☑ Step 2: Enable personalization and segmentation:
    - A. Define the data you want to segment and personalize with.
    - B. Design a form and save the URL.
- ☑ Step 3: Get an incentive:
    - A. Define a specific, actionable and immediate incentive.
    - B. Produce the incentive.
- ☑ Step 4: Deploy the opt-in form:
    - A. Pick the place and time to present your opt-in forms.
    - B. Choose a method to build and integrate your forms.
    - C. Design and deploy an opt-in form that converts.

6.9. How to design a space

"Have no fear of perfection -- you'll never reach it."

Salvador Dali

We all know what it feels like to walk into a well-designed space. Everything looks, feels and smells right. Somehow it invites you to stay.

Your store, bar or office are part of your Brand Experience.

These spaces should breathe your brand promise. That's what will get visitors to commit. Of course, the space will not do this by accident. Only if you design it to do so.

Your design decisions determine if visitors want to shop, eat or be employed there.

"This is the coolest place   "Yup."
to be an alcoholic."

And while there are many different ways to achieve this, there are some design principles and methods they share.

Let's explore:
- ✓ The rules for designing spaces.
- ✓ How to select a space.
- ✓ How to design a functional floor plan.
- ✓ How to source the elements.

The rules for designing spaces

Any space can be made to feel right using the following rules.

These rules don't guarantee magazine-level brilliance – but they'll (probably) prevent suicide fantasies.

"This office proves that life is pointless."

Adhere to these rules – they're the boundaries to observe when planning.

Now designing spaces is not an exact science. It's hard to tell when you've done a good job – since that's very subjective.

But if you'd love to spend time in your space, there's a good chance others might too.

It's the best benchmark to go by.

Include a threshold

Every space has a threshold area, or "decompression zone". These first 5 to 15 feet (1.5 to 5 meters) give visitors a chance to digest their new environment.

From here they will drink in your brand promise. How well thought out are your objects, textures, and colors? Do they want to spend their time or money here?

Keep the threshold open, inviting, and free of clutter.

Then, 90% of visitors turn right upon entering. The first wall in front of them is called the "power wall" and should contain your most important messages or merchandise.

Invest in the first wall to the right. It gets the most attention.

This is the place to tell your story or put your favorite fat margin products.

Prioritize light

Lighting is often an afterthought or something to consider if there's any budget left. However, lighting is crucial in building the right atmosphere.

If you can, try to pick a space with lots of natural light. It keeps people alert and happy. However, you can add to the natural light by using three types of artificial lighting:

- Ambient lights illuminate the space and set the mood, like ceiling lamps.
- Accent lights highlight artworks, shelves or plants, like spots.
- Task lights light workspaces, like table and bed lamps.

You can use these three to create light contrasts and inspire some playfulness. Don't go for uniformity. As for type: LEDs provide a better quality of light and save you money.

"This is nice and warm."

Include offbeat objects

For a space to be memorable, it has to be different. And the easy way to make a space different is to include some offbeat objects.

It's not about the functionality. It's about the feeling they convey that you're somewhere special. They are symbols.

- A ping pong or Fussball table is an anti-corporate statement.
- An aquarium signals exotic luxury.
- Metal posters with vintage prints indicate playfulness.
- Hammocks inspire adventurous apathy.

Try to find the offbeat objects that convey your brand promise.

Maximize livability

Don't choke your space.

Real estate is precious, and you want to use every last inch, but things need room to breathe. So don't saturate every piece of floor and wall. Keep it clean and spacious.

Add green.

Plants are beautiful and relaxing, as even the hardest cynic will admit. So why not decorate your space with lots of plants, flowers, and fresh herbs.

If you can't be bothered to maintain them, just get artificial greens. They go a long way in doing the same job.

Add texture.

Because the majority of walls are smooth - texture makes them interesting. A brick wall will destroy the monotony in a space, injecting some freshness.

Don't have a brick wall available? Don't fuss. Texture can be simulated with concrete, textured wallpaper, felt or murals.

Step 1: pick a space

The space you need will depend on your brand.

A. List your locations.

There are several ways to find suitable locations:

I. Search yourself. Real estate is listed online. As you search these online databases, list every location that's plausible enough.

II. Join an accelerator. Most major cities want to promote new business and rent refurbished locations to new businesses. They offer low prices and a sense of community.

III. Ask a realtor. She uses her knowledge of the market and connections to get you a list of spaces.

B. Score each location on the following parameters:

- **Cost:** Does it fit in your budget, or can you hardly carry the burden? Is internet, cleaning, and parking in the price included?
- **Proximity:** How important is being close to your customers and employees? What does it cost to be proximate?
- **Competitors:** Are there any vendors around that do the same thing? Will this impact your sales?
- **Appearance:** What are the boons of the space itself? High ceilings? Big windows? Modern toilets?
- **Size:** Does the space fit everything you want to do? How many desks or shelves do you need now and within the term of the contract?
- **Location:** What about the immediate vicinity? Dirty, dangerous or old-fashioned locations scare off customers and employees.
- **Access:** How easy is it to reach your place? Is there public transport and ample parking? Do you need a loading dock?

The wrong choice will give you headaches, so weigh these metrics well.

Make sure your evil lair has some privacy.

C. Negotiate the shortest rent possible.

If you're building a brand, make sure you can leave. You'll either grow too fast for the space to accommodate you or you'll fail. The space becomes a burden in both cases.

Step 2: Make a floor plan.

Large or small, you'll want to use your space effectively. You want to fit as many desks, shelves or racks as possible whilst keeping everything orderly and easy to navigate.

A. Make a list of all the desired elements.

List everything you'd like to have in your store. From chairs, booths, coffee machines, drapes, and duvets. From floor to ceiling and every wall.

B. Prioritize each element.

You are probably short on budget, space and time. So prioritize every item on your list with your team:

- **Must have:** What is critical to start using the space? For offices, this might be a number of desks and a meeting table. For stores, this could be a number of shelves and a check-out counter.
- **Should have:** What elements are important but not necessary for starting out? Think strategy boards for offices or mood-defining murals for stores.
- **Could have:** Things that will improve the experience. You get them when you have some spare time and money. Maybe that pingpong table?
- **Won't have (now):** Not important or appropriate enough. These elements do not add the value they cost and are abandoned for now. Perhaps next space.

C. Put your elements on a floor plan.

Putting things in a floor plan shows how the space is used. You can detect potential conflicts and cluttering before you get started.

If you want an impression of the mood, you can use a tool ⬤ that creates a shiny plan for you.

Step 3: source the floor plan

You're ready to source your floor plan. Start with the must-have items, then move down the list.

Starter budget

If you're broke or waiting to raise those millions before spending them, try:

- **Execution auctions** – Companies that fail or get their stuff repossessed auction off their inventory.
- **Second-hand sites** – Try putting together a semi-coherent batch of shelves or desks on a second-hand site like eBay or Craigslist.
- **Ali Express** – The Chinese will deliver you anything, fresh to the docks. You're rolling the dice though. The quality varies and returns are more expensive than your purchase.
- **Budget retailers** – Stores like Target have cheap furnishings.

Note that certain tax savings (VAT) don't apply when buying second hand.

"Looks like a million-dollar office to me!"

Regular budget

If you're swimming in opportunity but not in money, you might go to:

- **IKEA** – Great value for money, but should be mixed with other vendors to avoid that generic smell in your design.
- **Amazon** – Huge library of reviewed vendors for every product imaginable.
- **Etsy** – Unique and handcrafted items for every budget.

High-roller budget

If money is not a problem, neither is filling out your floor plan. Interior designers - who charge you to buy stuff with commissions - are happy to source your items. (Or heck, do your layout!)

If you want uncommon items, type in your item on Pinterest.

Queries like "Futuristic Wall Clock" or "Sleeping Pods" yield incredible results. Most of these are unavailable for sale, but you'll leave with a bunch of inspiration.

Step 4: publish your location

People are used to finding places by using Google.

A. Add your space to Google My Business

Your profile appears when people are searching for your business or similar business on Google Search or Maps. Upload some photos, your opening times and a description.

This is also a moment to reflect on how many stars you score on Google reviews and other review sites. Is it lower than nearby competitors? You'll be missing out on a lot of business. Start integrating ways to improve your social proof here.

B. Add your space to your website

Add your location and a nice photo. Companies housed in actual buildings inspire trust.

Summary and steps to designing your branded space

Your store, bar or office are part of your Brand Experience. And your design decisions determine if visitors want to shop, eat or be employed there.

You should design a space where you'd love to spend time by adding a clutter-free threshold, prioritizing light, including off-beat objects and maximizing livability.

- ☑ Step 1: pick a space.
    A. List your locations.
    I. Search yourself.
    II. Join an accelerator.
    III. Ask a realtor.
    B. Score each location on the relevant parameters.
    C. Negotiate the shortest rent possible.
- ☑ Step 2: Make a floor plan.
    A. Make a list of all the desired elements.
    B. Label each element must have, should have, could have or won't have.
    C. Put your elements on a floor plan.
- ☑ Step 3: Source the floor plan
- ☑ Step 4: Publish your location.
    A. List your space on Google My Business
    B. Add your space to your website.

6.10. How to make an app

"Design is not just what it looks like and feels like. Design is how it works."

Steve Jobs

Most brands have apps. For some, the app is the core of their business. For others, the app is just a loyalty instrument or a logistical tool.

And when I say 'app', I mean applications in the broadest possible sense: from browser-based desktop apps to mobile games.

Getting an app right is no small thing. If you want to hang on to your users, you have to provide intuitive structures and sexy looks across all platforms.

Both are the focus of an entire group of professionals, most of whom you can't afford.

Or maybe you can afford them, but you want to make effective use of their expensive time.

So let's take a look at how to do apps right in this chapter. We'll cover:
- ✓ The rules for designing spaces.
- ✓ How to select a space.
- ✓ How to design a functional floor plan.
- ✓ How to source the elements.

Rules for making apps

Most apps die off quickly because users don't stick around. The apps are not valuable enough or users don't discover this value before their patience runs out.

So absorb the following rules before designing your app. They'll prevent you from making the most common mistakes.

Usability first

Apps must offer a great user experience and an intuitive user interface.

In short, user experience (UX) is about the structure, where user interface (UI) is about the look. Think of it as putting sexy meat (UI) on sound bones (UX).

If you win at UX and fail at UI, your app is easy to use but looks terrible. If you win at UI but fail at UX, your app is hard to use but looks awesome.

UX is your priority. Your app should be usable by as many people as possible.

Most app designers are smarter than their users. That's why they often design apps that are too difficult for their audience to use.

Your app should be as easy as possible:
- ✓ **Less is more.** Use a clean interface with a minimum of elements needed to complete a task.
- ✓ **Use what they know.** Use buttons, icons, and names that users already know. The more familiar your design, the faster users learn to use it.
- ✓ **Make it predictable.** Users expect the things in your interface to behave a certain way. Make sure it lives up to it

Ease of use inspires further use.

Now what users find usable is not for you to decide. You might think your design is brilliant, but a user might find it frustrating:

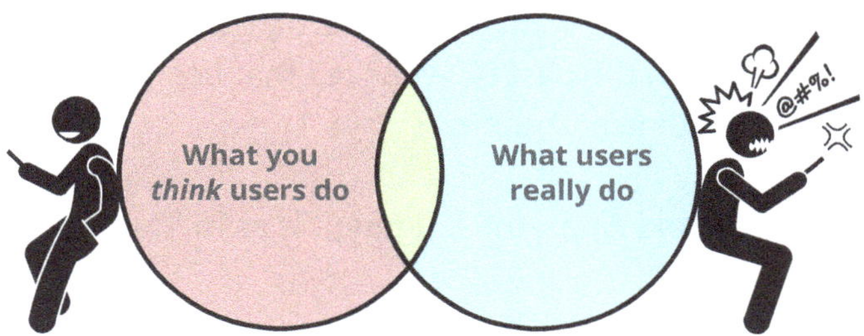

The reason for frequent user testing.

So don't be shy.

Put your app in front of users as soon as possible.

Preferably before it's built. Not after you've quit your day job and spend all your money.

Because there's a word for waging big money on dubious outcomes. It's called gambling. And as we'll see next, the odds are NOT in your favor.

"Put everything on 33!"   "Yes, sir!"

The crucial moment for your user is the sudden realization of your app's benefits. It's when she thinks: "Wow! This app is awesome!".

This moment should come as soon as possible because people are quick to abandon apps. We saw in the part on websites that users start out skeptical: is this really worth my time and energy?

Based on data on Android Apps, the judgment is as follows:[20]

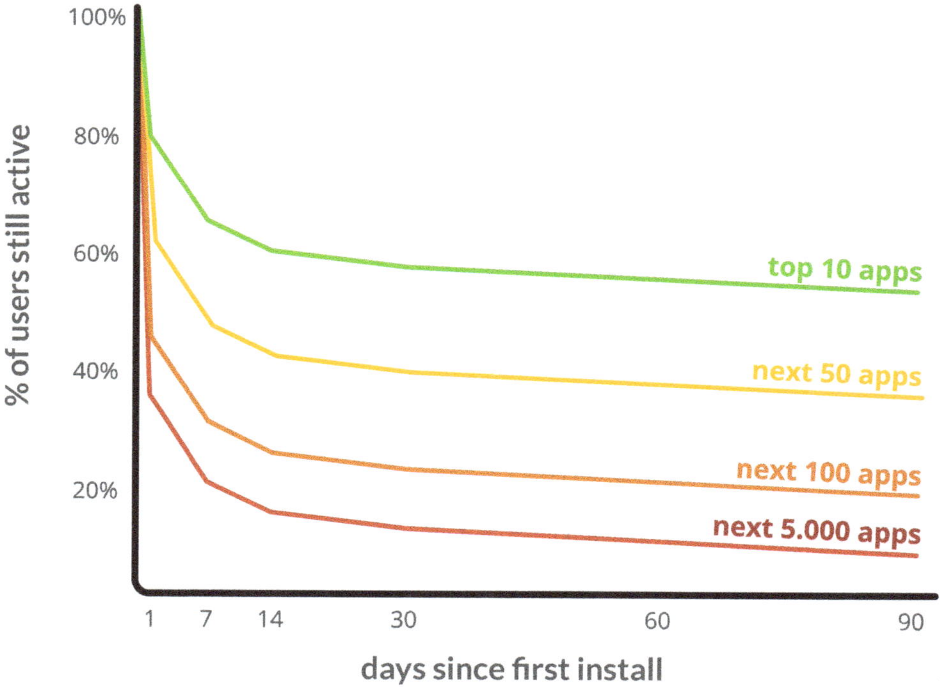

The more days pass, the more users bail. The vast majority of apps lose 60% within the first day and 90% within the first 90 days. Sad!

Only the top apps somehow manage to retain their users.

Why do their users decide to stay? That's easy. These apps are useful enough to spend time, energy or money on. The users think it's valuable.

So how do you copy their success? Simple:

Get your users to that moment where they experience the value of your app a.s.a.p.

- Is it blogging? Get users to write their first post. "Wow! I'm a blogger now." (Medium)
- Is it a social network? Get users to follow an X amount of people. "Wow! My feed is filling up!" (Twitter)
- Is it a website tracker? Get users to install the tracker on their website. "Wow! I can snoop on my visitors!" (Hotjar)
- Is it solar system design software? Get users to put down their first set of panels. "Wow! I can save time!" (Solar Monkey)

Design your UX so that users arrive at this pivotal moment as soon as possible. Lubricate the experience.

Radically cut the time and work required to get to the Wow! moment.

Want to know this moment for your app? You can find out in several ways:

- Ask your users: Why would you recommend us to friends? What do you like most about our app?
- Use tools ⊘ to record videos of user sessions. See where users bail.
- Users tools ⊘ to get usage data. What did users do in their first sessions? Which activities keep them coming back?

Onboarding means getting new users to understand and work with your app. You guide them to the Wow! moment and beyond. If you don't, users won't see the point of using your app and quit.

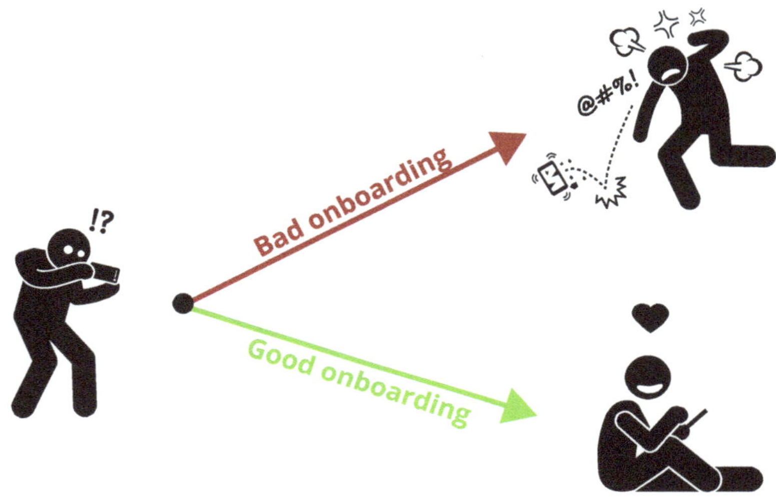

You can't have a successful app without good onboarding.

Now we all recognize the friendly screens, tooltips, visual cues and emails that help us navigate a new environment.

These are the best onboarding methods:
- **Showcase the benefits**: highlight the features or benefits of your app first. This motivates users to register with or learn your app.
- **Invite action:** Get the user to take a common action within the app, or have her take a series of them.
- **Setup the account:** If you need data or permissions from users before they can start using your app, it's wise to start with a simple, step-by-step setup.
- **Gamify:** Include a quiz or award points for taking certain actions.
- **Manual:** For expensive SaaS software it is common to get a walkthrough and setup help from a salesperson. If the money justifies it, you can offer in-app support.

Naturally, you can combine the above methods.

Now, what makes onboarding good?
- ✓ Keep it simple. People are busy.
- ✓ Use a minimum amount of words.
- ✓ Use simple visuals where possible.
- ✓ Use conversational language.
- ✓ One tip at the time.

So write down how you'd like to onboard your users. Feel free to take inspiration from similar apps – they've probably tested every route already.

Remember the goal: keep users coming back. Let them make a habit out of using your app.

Lets make it trump everything else!

The app design process

We saw that successful apps are usable, user-tested, and get to the Wow! moment quickly using onboarding.

With the rules in mind, we'll now design and build your app.

We'll use the following steps:
1. Ideation: Get all your ideas on paper and rank them.
2. Wireframe: Sketch the structure and screens of your app.
3. Prototype: Get a visual prototype of your app.
4. Build: Build your prototype.
5. Deploy: Deploy your app and acquire your first users. (Out of scope for this book)

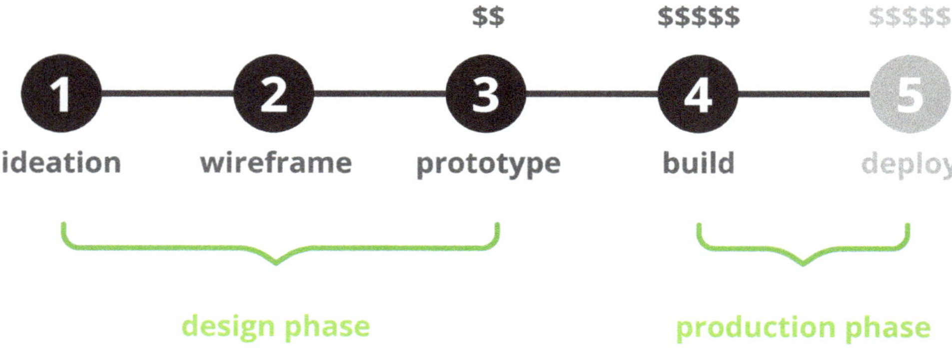

The design phase is cheap.

Things are done with pen and paper, or with easy tools. This is the moment to change your mind about your ideas, structure or design.

The production phase is expensive.

Changing your mind is pricy here. New builds and tests for all your devices and operating systems. Perhaps you need to spend fresh marketing dollars to get it adopted again.

Step 1: List your ideas and rank them with a GIMP

A. Write down all your ideas in a spreadsheet.

Everything remotely relevant is welcome on the list. Be exhaustive. Ask others for input also: your team, your neighbors or your boyfriend.

Sadly, you can't build everything on the list. With limited time, money, and user attention, prioritization is key.

B. Rank every idea on the list with a GIMP.[21]

GIMPing your ideas means scoring them from 1 to 10 for:
Gut – What does your instinct say about the value of this idea? Don't overthink it, just score it.
Importance – How relevant is the idea for the overall app experience? How useful will it be for your users? Will they adopt it quickly?
Money – How much resources will this idea demand? Will it add complexity? Security risks? Dependencies on third parties?
Probability – What's the chance that we're right? Are there any unknowns? What is the price we pay if it goes haywire? In short, what's the risk?

Got your scores? Good. Now multiply them to get your total GIMP score.

Gut x Importance x Money x Probability = GIMP score

Bring out the GIMP to score & rank your ideas

Angry GIMP
Score 0 - 600

Tepid GIMP
Score 601 - 4,000

Merry GIMP
< 4,000

You multiply them because a low scoring GIMP factor should drag down the entire idea. Needless to say, higher GIMP scores mean better ideas.

C. Select the best ideas for a minimum viable app.

By building this app you're making assumptions:
- The problem my app solves is pretty common (market size)
- People will definitely use this app to solve their problem (user adoption)
- My first users will be suburban moms (market segment)
- I will be able to charge money for my app (pricing)
- 50% of users will keep using it after installing the app (retention)

These assumptions might or might not be right. You better validate them with an app that delivers on the basics.

Get this minimal version out fast, then improve it with user feedback.

Use your best ideas, the merry GIMP's, to build the minimal version. The other ideas – including those users will give you – can be included (and scored!) later.

Step 2: Wireframe your app

Let's take the ideas you picked and sketch out how they'd look on a screen. This is called wireframing.

A. Sketch the screens of your app.

Simple lines, squares, and circles will do for now. Don't use colors, logos or other artwork. They distract from the purpose, which is deciding where things go, not how things look like.

- ✔ Make sure the users know what to next at all time.
- ✔ Show only what is necessary. Attention is scarce, so eliminate clutter.
- ✔ Every interface element should behave as you'd expect. What looks like a button should act as a button.

B. Draw arrows between the screens.

Now for the navigation. What does a click result in? Where does the user go? Which screen is next? Draw some arrows to indicate how the users travel between screens.

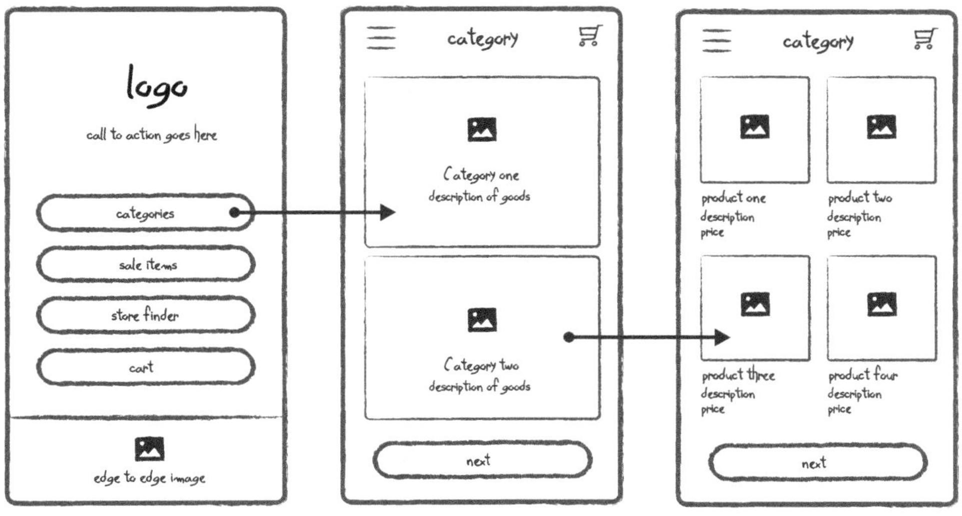

C. Evaluate your wireframe.

Your wireframes should portray a clear and coherent user experience. Because if the wireframe is already confusing, you'll build a Frankenstein of an app.

"Argh! The wireframe was off!"

For every screen, ask yourself:

- ✓ Is this screen serving the greater goals of the app?
- ✓ Is the purpose or task for this screen clear?
- ✓ Is it clear for users on how to act on this screen?

Don't forget to evaluate the total:

- ✓ Will this app be usable by every simpleton?
- ✓ How many steps to the Wow! moment?
- ✓ Where can I make it easier for the user?

The earlier you catch dubious layout and navigation choices, the cheaper. So don't continue until you feel your screen layouts are crystal clear.

Step 3: Prototype your app

You're about to spend the big bucks by building your app.

To make sure (1) the building goes as smoothly as possible and (2) the result is worth the money, you build a prototype of your app.

A prototype allows you to experience your app as if it was completed.

A prototype is more than just the design. It simulates the workflow, the interaction between screens and the overall look & feel without writing a single line of code.

A. Pick a prototyping tool.

There are many tools ⚡. you can use to build a prototype.

B. Design every screen.

Take the wireframes you built in the previous step and bring them to life by adding your logo, images, colors, and buttons.

Always check if your design is 'responsive' – if it looks good on different screen sizes.

C. Prototype the interaction.

Your wireframe defined the flow and paths of your app. Use your tool to define what user actions trigger app results like screen switches, color changes or animations.

D. Test your prototype with real users.

You'll now ask people to use your prototype and see if they encounter problems. So recruit some guinea pigs, watch them use your app, and take notes.

Can they do what you tell them to do? How long does it take them? Where are they confused?

Fail? Assume your app is stupid.
Not the users.

If multiple users experience the same problem, you'll have to fix it by changing the design.

There are two options for building your tested prototype:

Option I: Build it yourself (high skill or high budget)

If you are skilled enough – or got a serious budget, you can code it from scratch.

Whatever framework you use for building your app, there are manuals, libraries, and other resources to kickstart your project.

Hiring coders is expensive since they're in high demand. But perhaps you can ask for a fixed price if you completed the prototype.

Option II: Use an app builder (low skill or low budget)

Those with limited skills or budget can use an app builder. These are drag-and-drop tools that allow you to build your app without writing a line of code.

Needless to say, this severely limits what you can do with your app. But the results might be suitable as a minimum viable product.

Summary and steps for making an app

Making apps is about offering the user a great experience and a great interface. Your app should be easy to use (UX) and look awesome (UI).

- ☑ Step 1: List your ideas and rank them with a GIMP:
    A. Write down all your ideas in a spreadsheet.
    B. Rank every idea on the list with a GIMP.
    C. Select the best ideas for a minimum viable app.
- ☑ Step 2: Wireframe your app:
    A. Sketch the screens of your app. Include each idea.
    B. Draw arrows between the screens.
    C. Evaluate your wireframe.
- ☑ Step 3: Prototype your app:
    A. Pick a prototyping tool.
    B. Design every screen.
    C. Prototype the interaction.
    D. Test your prototype with real users.
- ☑ Step 4: Build your app:
    I. Build it from scratch (high skill or high budget).
    II.. Use an app builder (low skill or low budget).

Conclusion

"We got no troubles - life is the bubbles!"

Sebastian the Crab

That was it! You're a master now - able to build a complete brand that kicks ass and takes names. Please, feel free to wear a turtleneck.

Time to get sh*tfaced!

In time, your brand will get feedback. Friends will offer praise. Consultants will offer criticism. Yet only the opinion of your audience counts.

Your brand is good if your audience commits to your project.

The proof of your brand pudding will be sales, donations or votes. Nothing else matters. And since you read this book cover to cover – right? - you can't go wrong anymore.

Stick to your guns. Keep building. Keep testing. Keep winning.

Now if this book was useful to you, consider passing it to friends who dream of launching their own project. They need to convince a stubborn world and need all the help they can get.

If you loved this book, please let me know by reviewing it on Amazon, Goodreads, iTunes or where-ever you found it. It helps others discover the book and realize their dreams. (And yes, make me RICH!)

"IT WAS THE PLAN ALL ALONG!"

If you hated this book, please choke it down. I don't want the rating ruined by you sourpusses! Just ask for your money back at:
no-reply@brandbuilding.com.

Share your stories – be it glorious victories or crippling defeats –by sending me an email at wout@brandbuilding.com or tweeting to @chompff.

I'd love to hear from you.

Finally, let this end be a beginning. Of a successful brand, of a career as a brand builder, of discovering new ways to do things.

You're ready to dominate. Start polishing that cow. Go build your brand.

Appendices

A. How to brief a designer

Briefing designers is hard. Working with them can be too. They are a special bunch, often considering themselves artists. And artists have very strong opinions of their own work.

Some tips for working with designers

Designers want to make pretty things. But you want what's in the briefing. So box them in with clear instructions, and ask for regular updates. Prevent subsidizing some creative experiment. Never skip the intermediate checks by letting them dump a final design, for you will risk ruining the relationship and your budget.

As creative right-brain people, designers are often weak at negotiating, planning and conscientious delivery. You will have to manage them strictly. Let them know deadlines are important to you and hold them accountable if they bungle one.

Ask for multiple rough sketches to determine a direction together. When critiquing their work, mix in the occasional compliment. They often feel they wove threads of their soul into the fabric of the design, so never tear it down without ceremony.

Designers consider you illiterate in design and will claim to know best. Be patient with this. Acknowledge their input but stick to your branding strategy and identity.

What elements to include in the briefing

When briefing a designer, include a brand book that shows her what style to adhere to, like colors and logos to use. It will serve as an anchor.

If you don't have a brand book, make sure to add the following:
- The name of your business and organization
- Brand promise (E.G. my project is efficient, affordable and reliable.)
- Color codes
- Your industry (Beauty, Medical, Media)
- Specify the deliverable (file format, size, etc.)
- Define payment terms and milestones.

Improve your briefing by adding the following as well:
- Target audience demographics: Age, Sex, Location, Income, Occupation, Education, Industry
- Target audience psychographics: Interests, Lifestyle, Behaviour, Opinions, Values
- Add some images of other designs that you like to serve as a visual reference.
- Add your own ideas for this design (preferably in words AND rough sketch).

B. How to work with online freelancers

Online freelance platforms are awesome. For 10 years I delegated work that was either outside my skill set or that I wouldn't wish on my worst enemy.

Yet it isn't a magic arrow to get you retired early. Working with freelancers can be tricky. If you bungle it, you send the money for nothing and get sh*t for free.

Or you might miss crucial deadlines and lose your own customers. This guide helps you navigate that lucrative but dangerous landscape.

When should you use online freelancers?

Before you rise to the top of the corporate hierarchy or turn your business into a Google-size behemoth, you will have to delegate bite-size tasks. Freelancers can help.

They can assist you:
- When the job is menial and involves a lot of mindless repetitive work. Data checking, data entry, web scraping and the like.
- When you are busy and need some extra hands to do a task that you can perfectly do yourself. This means business is going well. Good for you.
- When the job is beyond your skillset. Perhaps you can't code as well as you told your client.

Know that option 3 involves danger since it's hard to judge work that you couldn't have done yourself.

Your freelancer might have smelled the weakness and will try to get you to sign off on sloppy work. She will point to the briefing and claim the work is done. This brings me to an important point:

Online freelancers will always choose the path of least resistance.

They will bury clumsy code where you won't find it. They will use workarounds instead of elegant fixes. They will misinterpret the briefing and hope that you won't complain. They will deliver half of work and pray you don't notice. And they can twitch like an eel in a bucket of snot if you try to get a grip.

Freelancers are not your employee. (Doh.) There are no promotions in it for them. Most assume this is a one-time thing and that you will never do business again. This incentivizes them to perform the minimum needed to receive their money and get a good rating. (More on this later.)

Of course, such behavior tends to fade as you build a relationship. But for now, I take it you're starting from scratch.

Which freelancers should you work with?

So why is there so much misunderstanding on deliverables? Freelance platforms are populated with people from cultures different from yours.

This means that besides different communication norms they also have different definitions of done. You might think an experienced freelancer can climb into your head and divine your wishes, but they can't.

Besides, they have no incentive to. They rather stick to your lousy briefing if that means less work. So remember:

The more exotic the culture of your freelancer (relative to yours) the more specific your briefing has to be.

If you want neat data, give them a template with some examples. If you don't, you'll get an Excel that looks like a madman's diary.

If you are asking for designs, send a bunch of references and specify your file type and resolution. If you don't, they'll scan used toilet paper and brag about art-deco creativity. (Ok, this is hyperbole.)

So don't skimp on detail. Read your briefing imagining you're the worst slacker on the internet. (Briefly. No need to become depressed.) Then scour your document again.

Find the holes in your briefing that can be filled with misunderstanding. Then plug them with more detail.

Now I will not recommend any cultures. That would ruin any political aspirations I don't have. But this is the internet, so let me share my experience and articulate it carefully:

Don't trust [expletive] [racial slur]!

Just kidding. You can try anyone from anywhere. I've had the best and the worst experiences on every continent. As with every business relationship, you will have to sniff each other out to ensure you are on the same page. So:

Start small and build trust.

Then take it from there. See if you grow into real partners. I have some guys and gals I've worked with since the beginning. Others I waved goodbye after the first dollop of work. Before you know it, you'll grow a circle of trusted allies that help you win big.

What to pay online freelancers?

If you are like me, you want everyone to get a fair share of the pie. You want long-lasting relationships with business associates you trust.

This attitude is great. You might even feel tempted to reward your freelancer royally for helping you with your project. After all, it's so cheap compared to what you used to pay!

But be disciplined. Perhaps you've never come close to hard labor. Maybe you feel tremendous guilt of paying these people peanuts. Don't.

Online freelancers love peanuts.

Don't believe me? Check the average salary in her country. It might be $100 a month. It might be $300 a month. You're probably crowning her queen of the neighborhood by paying what you pay.

But that's not the point. Paying more can be detrimental to the relationship. Because every bonus signals that you were willing to pay better. And every extra dollar means they lost a negotiation so brutally that you felt the need to compensate them.

Now the next time you bring work, she will up the ante and double the rate. And if you continue your redundant charity she might triple it.

The relationship is now less profitable for you, forcing you to abandon it and find a fresh one, uncorrupted by your habit.

You will incur the transactional costs of effort, time and risk as you build trust again. Needless to say, this is good for nobody. Remember:

Only pay more if it was more work than the briefing implied.

This is fair and keeps expectations clean as a whistle.

How to identify good online freelancers?

The moment you post a project online, you are swarmed with hungry workers. Most of them respond without even reading the briefing. So how to know which ones are good and which ones to avoid?

The best indicator for the experience of your freelancer is the number of projects completed.

But you want to check out their rating as well. With today's ratings, anything less than a perfect 5 stars means you're rubbish to work with.

This means that freelancers will do a lot to maintain their rating. Some can be pressured to upgrade their work by going the extra mile. Yet they also get to rate you as an employer.

And for you goes the same: anything less than 5 stars means that you're rubbish to work for. So it is in your mutual interest to be extremely clear in your expectations, but also forgive each other if the proverbial excrement ends up in the fan. So how about:

The best indicator for the quality of your freelancer is repeat hire rate.

Hiring someone again is the true sign that someone got value for money. Not the rating. This is because the (relatively rich) employers don't want to ruin their 5-star employer score for a few bucks. Disappointment is swallowed.

They curse their freelancer, vow to never work with her again, and then trade 5-star ratings just to burnish their own reputation. (Naturally, yours truly is the noble exception to this practice.)

C: On rasterized and vector image types

There are two image types you need to know about.
- Rasterized images (.JPG / .PNG)
- Vector images (.AI / .EPS / .SVG)

Rasterized images are made up of colored squares called pixels.

If you zoom in close enough at a rasterized image (Like a digital photo from your phone), it will look like a mosaic of squares.

- ✓ Easy to manipulate in Photoshop.
- ✓ Suitable for every purpose.
- ✗ Loses quality when scaled up.
- ✗ Large file size, even when optimized.

Vector images consist of points in space, connected to form shapes.

By coloring 2D points, lines and shapes you can create images without a lot of data.

- ✗ Hard to manipulate without some serious practice in serious software.
- ✗ Not suitable for photos or other realistic images.
- ✓ Scales without losing quality.
- ✓ Small file size.

Notes

1. https://www.statista.com/statistics/276703/android-app-releases-worldwide/
2. If you want to use my materials as an agency or educator, you'll have to contact me for a license.
3. Paraphrased from Plato's Apology 21a-d, 29a
4. And not just that cousin who tried a bike shop. Volkswagen blew millions on the Patheon.
5. Data from the World Database of Happiness, Erasmus University of Rotterdam, and the St. Louis Federal Reserve Bank.
6. Aronson, E., Wilson, T.D., & Akert, A.M. (2005). Social Psychology (5th ed.). Upper Saddle River, NJ: Prentice Hall.
7. Lee, Kwan Min (1 April 2004). "The Multiple Source Effect and Synthesized Speech". Human Communication Research. 30 (2): 182–207
8. Wooten, D. ReedII, A (1 January 1998). "Informational Influence and the Ambiguity of Product Experience: Order Effects on the Weighting of Evidence". Journal of Consumer Psychology
9. Liane Schmidt. (2007) "How context alters value." Scientific Reports volume 7, Article number: 8098
10. Joan Myers-Levy (2010) Journal of Consumer Research, Volume 37, Issue 1, 1 June 2010, Pages 1–14
11. Have a laugh. www.jonhaworth.com/toys/mission-statement-generator
12. http://simplicityindex.com/
13. Satyendra Singh, (2006) "Impact of color on marketing", Management Decision, Vol. 44 Issue: 6, pp.783-789
14. Steve Jobs paid Paul Rand $100.000 for his NeXT logo. And that's in 1986 dollars.
15. Courtesy of Mailchimp at https://mailchimp.com/why-mailchimp/
16. Courtesy of Pipedrive at https://www.pipedrive.com/
17. Courtesy of Intercom at https://www.intercom.com/
18. https://blog.hubspot.com/news-trends/content-trends-global-preferences
19. https://mashable.com/2016/06/15/facebook-video-five-years/
20. https://andrewchen.co/new-data-shows-why-losing-80-of-your-mobile-users-is-normal-and-that-the-best-apps-do-much-better/
21. Authors always come up with academic sounding acronyms. I wanted one of my own.

Lightning Source UK Ltd.
Milton Keynes UK
UKHW022330180223
417181UK00001B/70

9 789083 024929